The World of WINE

The World of WINE

FRANK E. JOHNSON

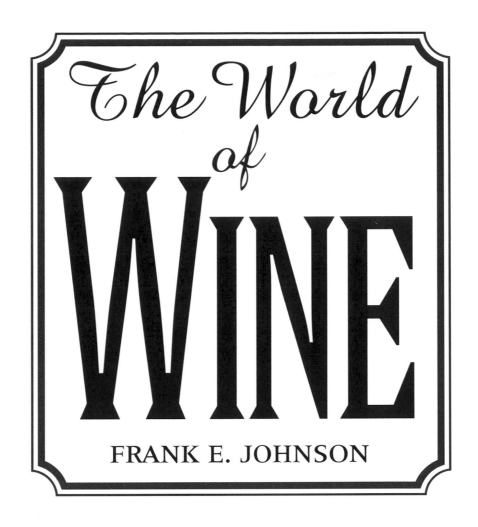

TIGER BOOKS INTERNATIONAL

This edition published in 1997 by
Tiger Books International PLC,
Twickenham, England

Produced by
Brompton Books Corporation
15 Sherwood Place
Greenwich, CT 06830

ISBN 1-85501-962-0

Printed in Spain

Page one: Ceretto cellars in Alba, in the Piedmont region of Italy. Ceretto was a pioneer in a softer, more accessible style of Barolo.

Page two: The Montepulciano district in Tuscany, Italy, at harvest time. Judging by the ripe bunches in the baskets, this appears to have been a good harvest.

Page three: Harvest in Puligny-Montrachet, France. Note that not all of these Chardonnay bunches are similarly ripe, but when pressed, the juice as a whole will be well balanced.

These pages: Inglenook vineyards in Napa, California, showing the springtime hues from wild mustard and the neat manner of training typical in Napa.

CONTENTS

INTRODUCTION

When I began collecting and writing about wines twenty-five years ago, there was a "standard literature" of wine reference books available. Works by André Simon, Frank Schoonmaker, Alexis Lichine, Harry Waugh, Edmund Penning-Rowsell and others focused on the same wines celebrated by previous generations of wine drinkers: château-bottled Bordeaux, Burgundy, Champagne, select German wines, vintage Port and Sherry. There was no need to expand beyond the standard literature on wine, because supplies were plentiful and the price of these exquisite wines, at the time, was still within reason.

All this changed in less than a decade. As many nations became more affluent, demand for the best known wines rose, along with the prices. It soon became clear that the standard literature on these wines was no longer adequate for the modern wine drinker. There was a wealth of new producers on the horizon,

as California wines came into their own along with many wines from Oregon, Washington, the American Northeast and Southwest, not to mention scores of fine Italian, Spanish and Australian wines. German wines and Portuguese rosés saw steady declines during the 1980s as White Zinfandels and "wine coolers" became more popular, along with South American wines. By 1993, Chile had displaced Germany to become the third largest exporter of wine to the United States – an event that would have been unthinkable twenty five years earlier.

Obviously these changes were driven by market forces, in addition to changing tastes. As the market expanded for quality wines, regardless of their source, it was plain that the standard literature was inadequate to properly trace their development. This book starts with a traditional perspective, and then goes on to highlight some of the new regions that

have graced the wine world during the past quarter century.

Dozens of excellent wine books and magazines have detailed these changes. But many of these contain more information than the average wine drinker is likely to use. Some of the wines they review are not widely distributed, or are prohibitively expensive for most people.

This book is different. In addition to listing the great wines that we often read about but seldom get to enjoy anymore, I have made an attempt to highlight many of the values that still exist in the wine world. All of the judgments and conclusions are mine alone, in large part compiled from over 10,000 tasting notes on wines from around the world. But above all, I encourage you to do your own experimenting and tasting.

Doing your own thinking is what this book is all about. As was my intent in my first wine book, *Professional Wine Reference*, I have always believed that people

Left: A typical Burgundy cellar, with new oak casks, in a vaulted cave.

Above right: Eduardo Chadwick, on his estate in Chile, with the foothills of the Andes in the background.

Below right: The Marquise Roussy de Sales, proprietor of Château de la Chaize in Brouilly, one of the leading properties in the Beaujolais district of France.

Below far right: Bringing in the harvest in Burgundy. Note that the weather is ideal; in many vintages, rain dilutes the crop and often causes rot.

enjoy things more when they learn for themselves, instead of following other opinions. Wine can be explained intellectually as well as by sensual experience, and the best way of describing it is with geography. So this book explores many of the world's major wine producing regions in some detail, complete with vivid photographs.

In the following pages you will encounter some terms that crop up frequently when describing vineyards around the world. One of the most important of these is "appellation," which is a fundamental part of most European wine laws. The English equivalent is place-name, meaning a plot of land with delimited boundaries that has been officially registered with the government. The concept of appellation is ages old in Europe, but relatively recent in the U.S. It specifies the right grape varieties (i.e. Cabernet Sauvignon, Chardonnay) for a specific area, fixes limits on yields (the amount that can be harvested), and standardizes grape growing and winemaking procedures. So far this has worked best within the European Economic Community (EEC), where mem-

ber nations have agreed to common winemaking standards; it is beginning to take hold slowly in the U.S., but much more needs to be done.

Wine is an immensely satisfying beverage – truly one of life's greatest pleasures. It was made to be enjoyed, savored, and shared with friends, and it

can be appreciated even more with a proper perspective on its origins. The following pages were written as your guide to the new world of wines – a world that has evolved well beyond the standard literature of the 1960s, and now beckons towards the next millennium. These are truly wines for the 21st century.

VINEYARDS

The vine responsible for all the world's best wines, Vitis vinifera – which includes thousands of different grape varieties – normally relies on a host plant or some other means of support. This means that while the vine can often stand on its own, depending on how and where it is grown, it must somehow be planted and trained so that the vineyard may be worked properly during the growing season.

Just as the gardener or orchard owner prunes his trees for optimum growth, a grape grower prunes the vines so the plant directs its efforts at bearing fruit. Pruning is performed during the winter, when the plant is dormant and there are no leaves; in the spring, at the beginning of bud break, the vine can be pruned further to regulate the size of the harvest.

Training is also necessary in many vineyards so that the developing leaves are properly exposed to the sun, and the grape bunches get some sunlight as well to assist in the ripening process. Training involves tying up or binding the vines to a means of support, with posts and wires, so that they line up in a row and can easily be maintained. The vines must be high enough to keep the grape bunches off the ground, where they would be susceptible to rot and disease, yet low

Left: Grafting vines in the Ribera del Duero area of Spain. This new region has witnessed extraordinary success with its wines in recent years.

Below left: Tinto Fino grapes in the Ribera del Duero area of Spain. These vines are trained fairly high to minimize the danger of rot.

Right: Pruning in Barbaresco, Italy, in February. Pruning is ideal under conditions like these, when the vines are dormant and covered with snow.

enough to allow the vineyard to be managed and trimmed of excess growth during the summer. In California and parts of the Rhône region in France, there are still some places where vines grow on their own, like little tree trunks, called head pruning. Another type of vine training used in some areas is the pergola system, or overhead trellis, whereby the vines are trained on overhead canopies to give a maximum exposure of sunlight to the leaves.

The way a vineyard is laid out depends on the soil, the exposure, the location, the climate, and the grape variety. If the land is flat and the soil is well-drained, vines can be arranged in neat rows so they can be easily worked by tractor and the grapes harvested by machine.

early in the day, or sometimes at night. Picking must be done rapidly but carefully; the bunches must be handled gently so that the fragile grapes do not shatter and promote spoilage. In the best vineyards, teams of highly trained pickers comb the vines and cut off the bunches with special shears. Elsewhere, this skilled labor can be done nearly as effectively by machine. The grapes are then brought to the winery as soon as possible, and are usually given an inspection to eliminate leaves and unripe or rotten berries. Harvest time is always a time for celebration; but it is also a time of hard work for the vintner. Tons of grapes arrive at the winery, and they must be quickly processed lest the grapes spoil.

Left: A very old vine in Provence, France, showing the result of many years of head pruning. In other parts of France this method is rarely used.

Above right: Spring leaves in Burgundy, France, near Aloxe-Corton. Growers' concerns over frost damage usually diminish after the middle of May, although in Burgundy it is a constant worry.

Above far right: Dan Duckhorn, of Duckhorn Vineyards in the Napa Valley, California, picking grapes to check sugar levels in the Three Palms Vineyard. Duckhorn is a small but very famous producer of Merlot.

Right: A picking team, ready for action. Plastic buckets and metal receptacles have now replaced the more romantic baskets in most areas.

This applies to much of California and Bordeaux. But if the land is steep and the soil is rocky, the vines must stand on their own, supported by stakes and not wires, and all work must be done by hand, as is the case in the northern Rhône in France and the Rhine and Mosel districts in Germany.

The annual life cycle of a vineyard progresses one day at a time. Even in the dead of winter when the vines are dormant, the vintner prunes for the future harvest. The first buds emerge in springtime, followed by the leaves; then in late spring the flowering takes place, which determines the size of the subsequent crop. Soon after the flowering, the first little grape bunches appear; green at first, then slowly changing their color as summer progresses. Little by little, the grape bunches get bigger and the grapes lower in acidity and get sweeter, if they are not destroyed by birds, deer or hail. Depend-

ing on conditions during the growing season, mold can break out in warm, humid weather and ravage much of the crop. To check it, the grower has to regularly spray the vines with sulfur, or, later in the season, with a copper sulfate/lime solution known as Bordeaux mixture or more advanced chemicals, which may be used selectively for certain diseases. But many environmentally-conscious growers prefer to use either the traditional measures or avoid the use of pesticides entirely.

As the grapes ripen on the vine, their sugar content increases as the growing season progresses. As harvest time approaches, the vintner measures the grape sugar daily from selected bunches. When they all indicate the desired degree of sugar, it is time to pick the grapes. Ideally, the harvest takes place under sunny conditions, but in some places daytime temperatures can be too warm, so picking is often carried out very

WINEMAKING

In many parts of the world, today's wine-making combines traditional craftsman-ship with modern winemaking tech-niques. Although most aspects of wine production have not changed much in over 2,000 years, cheaper and more effi-cient ways have been developed to process fresh grape juice.

At harvest time, fully ripened grapes have a sugar content of over 22% of their natural weight, and they will deteriorate if not processed directly. The alcohol in finished wine tends to act as a preserva-tive, and as the fermentation process burns up the sugar, the final result is a dry wine with a normal alcoholic content of about 12%. The noted French scientist Louis Pasteur (1822-1895) was the first to trace the process of fermentation in 1856, but the specific stages were only identified very recently. In essence, dur-ing fermentation the sugar molecule is broken down by yeast enzymes into smaller molecules of alcohol and carbon dioxide, with a considerable amount of heat given off in the process.

Winemaking techniques for red and

Above: Harvest at Casa Lapostolle in Chile. The protective barrier of the Andes in the background assures a regular harvest here.

Left: Picking time in Monthélie, Burgundy. Although most estates pick at the same time, very often the harvest is carried out in stages, owing to the weather.

Right: One of Bordeaux's most accomplished tasters and a world-famous wine maker, Jean-Claude Berrouet of Maison Jean-Pierre Moueix in Libourne, France, samples some of his wares.

My favorite advice to new wine tasters is: no one was born with a silver grape in his mouth. Wine tasting involves much of the same techniques as tasting food or any other beverage: it demands your full attention, and a certain memory for flavors, but there really isn't anything special about it. You probably already know much more about wine tasting than you think. But there are a few rules to follow.

In order to properly judge a wine, first select an appropriate glass. Most wine glasses, including those used in restaurants, are designed to stand up to rough handling, and do not present the wine properly. Ideally, the glass should be shaped like a tulip or a chimney, narrowing at the top. For tasting purposes, the glass should never be filled more than 1/3 full, to allow it to aerate properly.

Next, take a good look at the wine. A young white should be limpid, clear and have a pale straw color; if it is deep golden or brownish, it is probably too old. A young red should be bright purple or ruby; older red wines turn a brick-red color as they age in bottle. The wine should also be clear, and if it is cloudy, the wine may not have been filtered. With some wines, this is not a defect; with others, it may mean that the wine has been stored improperly at some point before you bought it. Always buy your wine from a reputable wine merchant.

Then, move the wine around in the glass, with a swirling motion. Place the

Wine Tasting MADE SIMPLE

Many people are afraid to taste wine. After being exposed to the mysteries and ritual of wine tasting, perhaps after being handed a wine list filled with unfamiliar names, they think that they aren't properly qualified to judge a wine – and even if they are, they lack the experience to enjoy it.

glass on a flat surface and rotate it with the stem between your fingers, moving the glass counterclockwise. You will see the wine begin to coat the inside of the glass. Next, take the glass and bring it to your nose.

Now is the time to appreciate the bouquet which is the scent a wine gives off when aerated in this fashion. Don't take a giant sniff – take a whiff or two, slowly. Swirl the glass again, and sniff the wine again. It should have a vinous aroma, but if it has been in bottle for several years, it should show the complex nuances of bottle bouquet, which relates to any fine wine that has been properly stored. The bouquet of a wine is a powerful clue to its quality. Certain grape varieties give off a powerful grapey scent (Muscat, Gewürztraminer); this is not the same as bottle bouquet because it is unrelated to aging.

Sniff the wine. Does it have a grapey scent, or is it more floral? Wine grapes have a special ability to mimic other fruits and flavors: is there a scent of ripe peaches or apricots (Chenin Blanc, Riesling)? In certain red wines, do you pick aromas of cherries or plums (Pinot Noir, Merlot) or chocolate or menthol (Cabernet Sauvignon)? Try and characterize what you are smelling so that you can better remember the qualities of the wine.

Now sip. Roll the wine around on the palate, giving it the maximum opportunity to show its body, its depth of flavor, and its overall quality. Is it sharp or smooth? Is it a wine you would enjoy right away, or would it be better in an other year or two? Now would be a good time to write down some impressions and plan for future enjoyment.

white wines are not the same. The primary difference is that red grapes are crushed, so that the juice remains in contact with the skins during fermentation and hence has a chance to extract the color; white grapes are generally pressed whole and the juice ferments separately, away from the skins. A rosé or blush wine is essentially a red wine that has been given only limited skin contact (one day or less).

The yeast involved in winemaking is the species Saccharomyces cerevisae, which is one of a group of yeast plants that will ferment grape sugar and transform it into wine. Traditional wine regions have long relied on indigenous wine yeasts, naturally occurring on the "bloom" or surface of the grapes, to start fermentation. The age-old practice of returning winemaking remainders as fertilizer in many traditional vineyards allowed a natural buildup of desirable yeasts over the years. Newer winemaking regions do not normally have this concentration of beneficial yeasts, and selected yeast strains have to be inoculated (added) for fermentation to occur.

Associated with the process of selected yeast inoculation is a dose of sulfites, from the addition of sulfur dioxide

as a sterilizing agent, just prior to fermentation to eliminate unwanted wild yeast and insure that only the right yeasts are present to do the job. Again, many wineries are abandoning this practice, in efforts to lower the levels of sulfites in finished wines. In the U.S., concerns over sulfite levels in wines and their possible effect on allergies led to the enactment of sulfite warning labels in 1987, followed by more specific warning labels relating to alcohol abuse. As a consequence, much lower levels of sulfur are normally used today, at least in this initial stage.

Fermentation results in the liberation of a great deal of heat, and heat itself speeds up the process, much like a nuclear chain reaction. If left unchecked, rapid fermentation results in dull, flawed wines, so the winemaker has to have some means of controlling the temperature. Today, there are several means available: 1) constructing the fermenting vessel of stainless steel, which gives off heat naturally; 2) using a heat exchanger, either in the form of an internal coil in the fermenting tank or a series of fins on a radiator, through which the wine may be drawn or pumped, so that the heat is given off; 3) water cooling, sprayed over the outside of the tank; 4) refrigeration

of the fermenting must through mechanical means. All four of these methods came into widespread use only during the last twenty years. Their initial benefit was a major improvement in many white wines, which need proper temperature control to preserve their freshness, but the system brought major benefits to fine red wines as well, whereby the rate of fermentation could be closely monitored

Above left: Picking Chardonnay in Napa, California. In warm areas like Napa, harvesting begins very early in the morning to minimize spoilage by heat.

Left: A metal screw, made of stainless steel gently moves ripe Chardonnay grapes to the presses.

Above: Penaflor winery in Argentina is one of the nation's largest, with its automated facilities for processing the grapes.

Right: Finca Flichman winery in Mendoza, Argentina, where stainless steel fermenting tanks, introduced over the years, have greatly improved the quality of the wine.

during the several weeks they require for skin contact.

In earlier times fermenting vats were usually made of wood, which was readily available but made temperature control and cleaning difficult. Nowadays stainless steel is the material of choice, but for certain grape varieties barrel fermentation gives better results. The use of new oak barrels gives off valuable flavor enhancements, and the limited contact with oxygen found in the wood pores adds complexity to the flavor. There is an added benefit, in that the wine may be stored in the barrel after it is fermented.

Once the yeasts assimilate all the sugar, the cells settle to the bottom of the barrel and eventually die. The concentration of dead yeast cells and wine remainders is known as "lees," and in recent years winemakers have determined that for certain wines, contact with the lees over a period of several weeks improves the flavor. This technique, known as "sur lie" aging, is native to the Muscadet area in France but has become popular in many other wine regions.

The first fermentation is alcoholic, resulting from the action of yeast. A second, bacterial fermentation can take

place later, which is called malolactic fermentation, after the lactobacillus or leuconostoc bacteria that carry it out. Unlike alcoholic fermentation, which converts sugar to alcohol, malolactic fermentation changes the sharp malic acid in young wine to lactic acid, which is softer, giving off a measure of carbon dioxide in the process. Malolactic fermentation may occur naturally and spontaneously or may be induced artificially, with the proper bacterial culture. The effect of malolactic fermentation in a Chardonnay can be determined by a noticeable flavor of butterscotch, and a soft, smooth texture on the palate; if this flavor is overly pronounced then the winemaker has used too much malolactic fermentation.

Sparkling Wine

All wines give off carbon dioxide and alcohol when made, but with still wines the gas is allowed to escape. If a second fermentation can be introduced, in a sealed vessel, the wine can be made sparkling. The trick is to select the right blends of still wines that are low in alcohol to begin with. As practiced in Champagne, the best and most costly method

Above: American oak vats at Vega Sicilia, the producer of Spain's rarest and costliest red wines.

Left: A cross section of a cask at Château du Cléray, Muscadet, France, showing the lees as sediment on the bottom of the barrel where wine is aged. This sur lie technique is widely used for the best Muscadets.

Right: Christophe Magimel, assistant cellarmaster, performs the racking (soutirage) at Château Latour in Bordeaux.

Above far left: Riddling by hand (remuage) at Perrier-Jouët, Champagne, the traditional method for clarifying Champagne. Today, more and more riddling is done by machine.

Left: Modern riddling equipment at Domaine Chandon in the Napa Valley, California.

Above left: Disgorging (dégorgement) or removal of the sediment at Champagne Barancourt, showing the box used to protect workers from defective bottles.

Above right: A modern bottling machine, designed to fill bottles in a circular motion in order to keep the flow constant.

is to carry out the second fermentation in bottle, over a period of months. This "méthode champenoise" has been in use for centuries, and until recently involved a lot of hand labor. The process involves adding a sugar and yeast solution to a pre-selected wine, known as the bottling dosage or "liqueur de tirage," and then sealing it in bottle so that the second fermentation can take place.

Once fermentation is finished, the dead yeast cells fall to the side of the bottle; because the wine is sparkling, they are easily stirred up when the bottle is opened, making the wine cloudy and unattractive. So a way has to be devised to separate the yeast cells from the wine. About two centuries ago, the technique of remuage (riddling) was developed to remove the yeast. The bottles are carefully rotated over time, at different angles so that eventually the bottles stand on end, with all the yeast accumulated at the cork. Then, the bottles are taken to a freezing brine bath, where the neck is frozen and finally the wine is uncorked or "disgorged" – out pops the frozen sediment, with only a small loss of wine or pressure. Until recently, this entire process had to be carried out by hand, which was a major factor in the high price of Champagne. Now much of the process can be automated. Riddling racks have been replaced in many cellars by mechanical vibrators, and even the disgorging process can be done by machine.

Earlier in this century, the Transfer

Left: Frozen bunches of grapes await harvesting, at the very end of the vintage, to be used in a rare German dessert wine, Eiswein.

Right: Manzanilla, the lightest and driest of Sherries, served in the traditional copita glasses of the Andalucia district of Spain.

Process was developed in Germany to eliminate riddling and disgorging. In transfer, all of the steps are the same as the méthode champenoise, up until the time of riddling. Instead of being put on racks, the bottles are attached to a transfer machine, whereby the wine is automatically filtered and rebottled in a short period of time.

If the benefits are so obvious, why hasn't this process displaced the traditional méthode champenoise? Because of the precise degree of control in the riddling method, and the inevitable loss of some pressure during the time spent in the transfer machine, the Champagne method is still preferred. The sparkling wines prepared by transfer are qualitatively in the middle rank, while the following process for sparkling wine is more appropriate for lesser wines.

Around 1910 Jean-Eugène Charmat, a Frenchman, devised a process for making large quantities of sparkling wine in only a matter of days. The process, known as Charmat or bulk process, uses a set of tanks where wine is artificially aged by heating, then given a second fermentation. Pressure building up in the tank makes the wine sparkle on its own, and after about a week the wine is filtered and bottled directly, with no bottle fermentation taking place at all.

While Charmat process wines are popularly priced, they cannot compare with those that have been bottle-fermented. The reason is that after the second fermentation, the long association between alcohol and carbon dioxide in the bottle results in a new molecule entirely – allowing the wine to stay sparkling for much longer and to give off small, refined bubbles that persist in the glass. Ultimately, it all depends on what the winemaker, and the consumer, wants to spend.

Fortified Wines

Fortified wines are those to which brandy or spirits have been added. Adding brandy serves one of two purposes: 1) raising the alcoholic content; 2) stopping fermentation, by raising the alcoholic content above the level where yeast can do its work, thereby retaining the original sugar in the grape must. Broadly speaking, we can say that the first method applies to the Sherry district, and that the second process is used in making Port. The technique was developed about 500 years ago to stabilize wines, when wine traders were concerned that they would not withstand temperature extremes during long ocean voyages.

Late Harvest Wines

In simple terms, a late harvest wine is made from grapes picked later than usual. Depending on the weather, grapes can continue ripening well after the normal harvest time, to become overripe. The timing for picking is very important, because the plant can quickly start drawing back the grape sugars as it shuts down for the season. In dry, sunny vintages where frost is not a problem, late harvested wines are common.

But another type of late harvested wine relates to a mold, known technically as Botrytis cinerea, which is only found in certain areas – most notably river regions, where certain climatic conditions exist. In the right vintages, where warm temperatures and high humidity continue late in the growing season, Botrytis develops on grapes and often on entire grape bunches. If rain or birds do not interfere, Botrytis shrivels the grapes and concentrates both the sugar and the acidity – a phenomenon unique to this type of fungus, and to certain grape varieties that have the sort of skin and primary flavors that are enhanced by the action of the mold.

In traditional areas, such as the Sauternes and Barsac districts of Bordeaux, plus Quarts de Chaume and Bonnezeaux in the Loire, Botrytis is called "pourriture noble," or noble rot, based on its importance in the production of sweet wines. Sweet wines can be made without Botrytis, and in fact most sweet wines are – but in great vintages the mold transforms the ordinary grape flavors into luscious combinations of honey and ripe fruit, adding a flavor all its own.

Ice Wine

If the harvest is allowed to extend very late in the growing season, to the point where frost sets in, another type of late harvested wine can be made when the grapes are partially frozen. Known as Eiswein, these are sweet wines that come from grapes gathered very early in the morning, when the water in the grape has frozen but the sugar and acidity has not. The grapes are picked rapidly, and pressed before the grapes have had a chance to thaw. A sweet elixir is extracted and fermented to make ice wine.

Eiswein production is a rather new development. It only became commercially popular in the 1960s with the advent of a new pneumatic press, known as the Willmes press, which through its design (an inflatable bladder encased in a slatted cylinder), allows frozen grapes to be gently and precisely pressed. This was very difficult, if not impossible, with older vertical presses used until recently in many cellars; as a result, today many more growers in Germany, and throughout the world, are making ice wines.

WINE ACCESSORIES

The first wine glass was probably a pair of cupped hands. A lot has happened since then, as wine drinkers over the centuries learned that in order to properly appreciate a good wine, there must be some way to influence its appearance, its temperature and its rate of evaporation. In recent years there have been many new storage systems, cooling devices and glassware that accomplish this goal.

Wine storage

For those who purchase young wines and intend to lay them away for several years, some means of temperature control has to be in place so that the wine will improve with age and not spoil because of temperature variations. Wines age best in a cool, dark place with a constant temperature and humidity, such as basements constructed deep underground – provided that the wine is well removed from a furnace or a hot water heater.

The ideal temperature for long term storage is about 55 degrees Fahrenheit; colder temperatures will delay the aging process, while warmer temperatures will hasten it. A constant temperature is vital; it is better to age wine in areas that are warmer than 55 degrees but stay constant throughout the year, rather than in a place where the temperature may be cool initially but will vary considerably later on. All bottles should be stored in the horizontal position, so that the corks stay moist and keep air out of the bottle.

The old conception that a spoiled wine "turns to vinegar" is not entirely accurate. While vinegar bacteria can contaminate a bottle once it is opened, wine that is exposed to heat and temperature fluctuations while in the bottle is said to be "heat abused," and has a cooked, sherryish flavor as opposed to the harsh, acidic taste of vinegar. A wine will rarely turn vinegary unless it is opened.

In recent years, electronic storage sys-

Left: Wines from Viña San Pedro, Chile, with the vines and the Andes serving as a backdrop.

Right: This electonic wine storage system allows for a temperature controlled wine cellar in the living room.

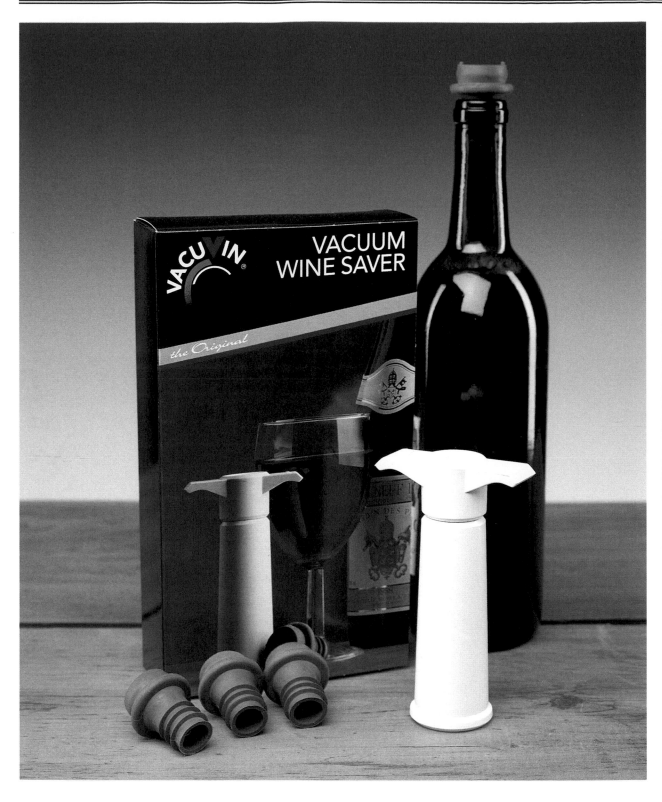

tems were developed that allow people with limited space a means of temperature and humidity control. These systems may range from small enclosures capable of only holding a few cases, to elaborate walk-in systems with a capacity of hundreds of bottles. There are also a number of elegant wine racks available for storage. But you don't have to spend a lot of money to lay down your wines. The wooden boxes that come with better Bordeaux and Burgundies constitute an excellent temporary storage medium. They are already equipped with slats in place for the bottles, hold up very well to mold and humidity, and can be sealed to minimize temperature variations.

Another, more permanent approach to laying away wines can be made with inexpensive clay pipe sections, available from commercial plumbing supplies or lumber yards. They regulate temperature since they are insulated and help keep the wines cool.

Above: The "Vacu-Vin" is a handy way to keep wine fresh overnight with its one-way valve that sucks and keeps oxygen out of the bottle.

Right: A selection of the wine openers available today.

Coolers

The old fashioned wine cooler was practically synonymous with decadence. Made of silver or glass, it held a generous portion of ice intended to chill even the most reluctant bottle of Champagne, and it wasted a lot of water.

Some wine books warn against putting wine in the freezer, yet this has essentially the same effect as putting a bottle in an ice bucket, without wasting water, except for the additional 10 or 20 degrees of chill that can freeze the bottle if left there too long. Placing the bottle sidewise on a tray of ice also speeds up the process.

There is a new, inexpensive device now available for chilling wines called the "Rapid Ice," consisting of a circular plastic wrapper with segments of liquid gel. All you have to do is keep the chiller frozen until ready to use, then slip it over the bottle and in five minutes the wine will be ready to serve and will stay cool at the table.

Left: "Rapid Ice" is an inexpensive device for cooling white wine in just five minutes.

Below: The executive tasting room at Sebastiani in California. Wine professionals use spittoons to avoid consuming too much wine during tastings.

Right: The "Private Preserve" system keeps opened bottles fresh by pumping in nitrogen from an aerosol tank.

Stoppers

Getting the cork out of a bottle is only half the solution. What happens when you want to recork the bottle for another occasion, and then find that the cork won't fit?

The easiest solution, for those who consume Port, Sherry and brandy on occasion, is to save the small corks that come with these bottles. But because the wine still is in contact with the air, this solution works only for a day or two, then the wine gets stale. Two methods have been developed to counter the spoilage problem: first, by removing the air through a vacuum pump, and second, by storing the wine under a blanket of inert nitrogen gas. The most popular brand in the first group is probably the "Vacu-Vin". The "cork" is actually a rubber seal with a one-way valve, and when fitted to the pump, the Vacu-Vin draws the air out of the bottle. The Vacu-Vin is a handy way of keeping wine fresh overnight. But it can also pump out valuable aromas and essences if it is used too many times on one bottle.

There are some other home wine dispensers available that keep air from spoiling wine once it is opened. A cheap solution is the "Private Preserve," which consists of a simple push-button aerosol tank, filled with nitrogen and fitted with a plastic probe that inserts in the bottle after opening. The Private Preserve then evacuates air out of the bottle and floods the air space in the bottle with a protective blanket of gas.

Keeping Champagne from losing its bubbles after opening is a major concern since ordinary corks can pop out of the bottle under pressure. A way to minimize bubble loss is to keep sparkling wines thoroughly chilled at all times, in an ice bucket. Ideally, you should get a specialized champagne cork, which is an oversized metal stopper that fits over the bottle with clamps. These devices work quite well, and are inexpensive and readily available.

Corkscrews

The corkscrew is an important part of what is called the "ritual of wine." The basic design of most corkscrews has not changed in hundreds of years, although recently there have been a few improvements to make them easier to use.

There are actually two tasks associated with wine openers: cutting the foil capsule surrounding the top, and extracting the cork. The simplest corkscrews just have a spiral fastened to a handle, and there is no means of taking off the foil capsule. But the most common corkscrew, the "waiter's" corkscrew, has three segments: a central spiral that unfolds in use; an end hinge for leverage, and a small knife for cutting the foil. The corkscrew folds up and can easily be carried around in a pocket. It is known as a waiter's corkscrew because it is usually simple and cheap enough for waiters to keep one on them at all times.

A better design is a double-action corkscrew, which has two sections that move in different directions. The central portion moves the screw itself, until it is seated all the way into the cork. The outer portion is then rotated and lifts up the central section, gently but firmly extracting the cork from the bottle. Because there is little or no shaking associated with this corkscrew, the double-action corkscrew is especially well-suited to serving older wines that may have sediment and have to be carefully handled before they are decanted.

One of the best recent corkscrew designs is the "ScrewPull", designed by an American inventor. It actually combines the actions of a wing-type corkscrew with a double-action device: one merely places the device over the bottle, then engages the screw and turns its handle until the unit's design slowly draws out the cork in a continuous motion. It is simplicity itself.

Glasses

The beautiful crystal glasses and stemware often seen in old family heirlooms and museums were designed by glassmakers who probably drank no wine themselves. These glasses were crafted for their visual appeal, and provided little or no conditioning of wine. A perfect example is the old fashioned wide "champagne glass," quite common at the turn of the century, which allowed a glass of sparkling wine to go flat in a matter of minutes.

The concept of matching a wine to a specific glass is not new: formal dinners many centuries ago featured a number of different glasses to accompany each course. But the concept of optimizing a wine with a specially shaped glass is quite new, since many of the world's established glassmakers have traditionally stressed beauty before functionality. Smaller glasses often lack a proper flute shape, which acts as a chimney to develop the bouquet; larger glasses may flare out at the sides, and thus fail to concentrate the wine's scent.

Today's wine glasses are designed to take into account the differences between red, white and sparkling wines. White wines, because they are served

Left: A sommelier in a top flight French restaurant, decanting an older Bordeaux into a crystal decanter by candlelight. This age-old method clarifies and aerates the wine.

Above right: Georg Riedel, managing director of Riedel Crystal of Kufstein, Austria, showing his range of glasses designed to specially condition each type of wine.

chilled, can be served in small glasses but they must be tapered to show off their delicate aromas. Red wines need a larger bowl, either in a balloon or a tulip shape, to be swirled and release the ripe scents of bottle bouquet. Sparking wines need a long, graceful flute-like glass to show off the bubbles as they rise; this design also helps keep the wine cool and consequently retains the bubbles for a longer period of time.

One of the early pioneers in specialized wine glassware was Claus Josef Riedel of Austria, who in the 1950s experimented with machine- and hand-blown glasses to determine the proper shapes for conditioning various wines. Out of his experiments came a whole series of differently shaped wine glasses, optimized for Bordeaux, Burgundy, Rhine wines, sparkling wines and brandies. One of his designs, the Sommelier Grand Cru Burgundy series, was so innovative that it is now on permanent exhibit at the Museum of Modern Art in New York.

Riedel glasses are probably the most famous of the group, but they are by no means the only wine glasses worth buying. Competitive designs have recently been offered by many other glassmakers, and they all work in similar ways to condition different wines. Regardless of the brand you prefer, there are a few rules regarding proper wine service:

● chill the wine slightly before service. All whites and many red wines improve when refrigerated for a few minutes.

● never fill the glass more than $1/3$ to $1/2$ full, so you can swirl and sniff the wine before drinking which enhances the tasting experience.

● swirl the wine before sipping it to release the bouquet in the glass, either on its base or by tilting the glass and moving it slowly.

● decant an older wine into a decanter, or a clean, washed bottle, to remove it from its sediment. Decanting may also aerate a younger wine and allow it to "breathe." Opening a red wine a few minutes before service may serve the same purpose, but decanting will usually do a better job.

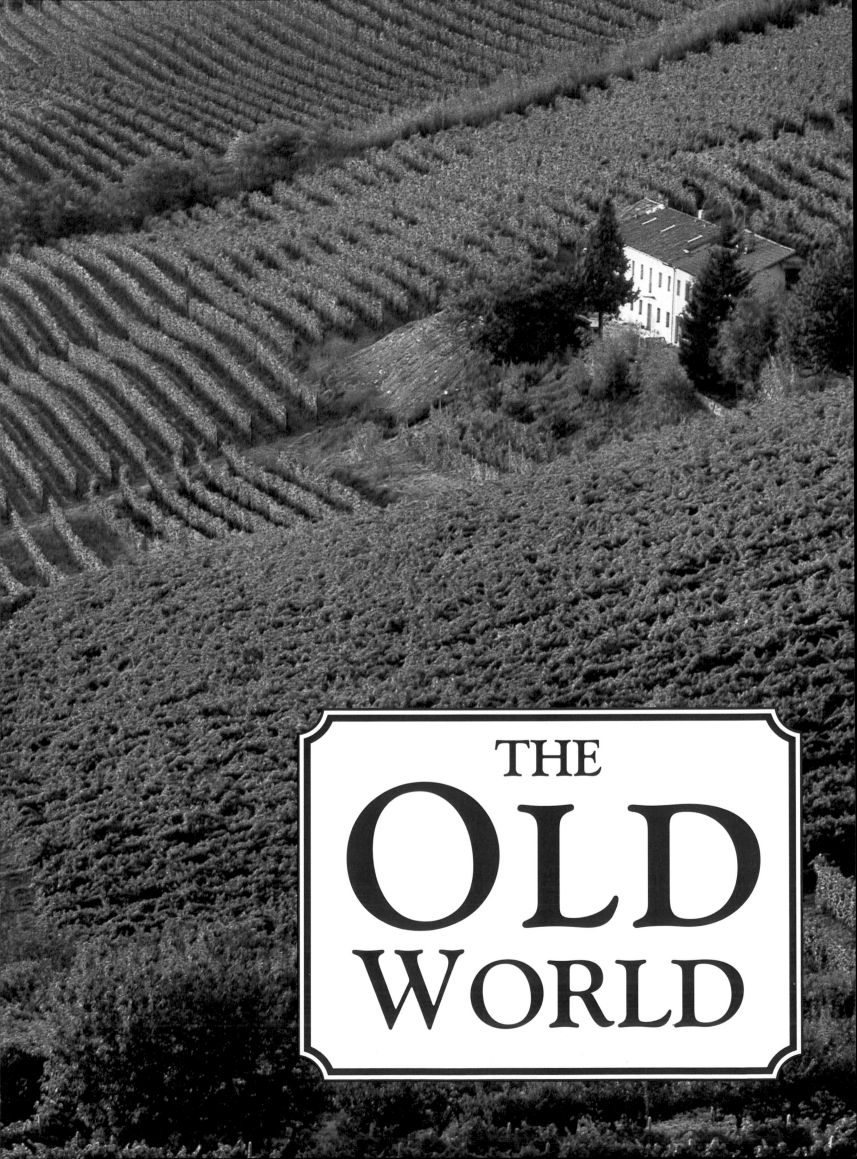

THE
OLD
WORLD

FRANCE

In a tradition dating back thousands of years, France has probably spent more time promoting quality wine than any other wine-growing nation. While many other countries grow wine in abundance and have similar quality traditions, France has been more thorough in identifying them, highlighting their virtues, and making them available on a regular basis.

There are several factors that make French wines so important. The first is the French themselves. Wine drinking is a normal and accepted part of everyday life in France and a natural part of a healthy lifestyle, underscoring the importance of wine consumption in moderation. Another factor relates to France's geographic location. From the cool northern vineyards of Champagne down to the sunny Mediterranean, the vine has a nearly ideal home throughout much of the country, with regular sunshine interspersed with seasonal rainfall, giving consistently fine results.

There are officially four quality categories for wines in France. The first is simple Vin de Table (table wine), sold without any indication of origin. This accounts for the vast majority of wine sold in France itself, and is the most basic wine exported. The second group, Vins de Pays, or country wines, is a fairly broad category of wines sold under regional names, which allows some blending. There are dozens of these Vins de Pays now on the market; some of them are quite good and are usually quite inexpensive. The third category, known as V.D.Q.S. or Vins Délimités de Qualité Supérieur includes smaller wine districts superior to Vins de Pays. Under the system, the wines can be reclassified to a higher quality level, once they have shown continued improvement.

After several hundred years of relying on local wine laws, France passed the appellation d'origine contrôlée (A.O.C.) laws in 1935, which relate to the fourth and highest quality level of French wine. The term means "controlled place name of geographical origin," indicating that a wine is sold with the name of its vineyard and growing district. A major part of the appellation contrôlée laws relates to controlling production, to insure that quality standards for the best wines will always be upheld. The laws provide for an escalating quality scale, in which yields for the best wines are deliberately kept low to assure their consistency. This measure came about in the 1970s after several abundant vintages flooded the market with light, uninteresting wine that had to be sold at a loss.

Importantly, the appellation contrôlée laws also mandate the grape varieties, vine training systems and production methods for each area. They also establish the location and exact boundaries of each French vineyard, which will be sold under appellation contrôlée.

Previous pages: Barbaresco vineyards in Piedmont, Italy, showing the characteristic steep terrain of the region.

Left: Chevalier-Montrachet, accessible by ancient walls, is a famous vineyard in Burgundy, France.

Above right: Burgundian workers, with a pitcher of wine after a hard day's work.

Below right: Château Lafite-Rothschild, from the "route des grands crus" in the Médoc. This building is the central cellar; the vineyards are out of sight in the background.

❧ Burgundy ❧

Along a narrow ribbon of vineyards, flanking the broad valley of the Saône to the east and the hills of Haut-Bourgogne, some of France's most highly prized wines are grown. This "slope of gold," or Côte d'Or, has been famous for its wines since the middle ages – and the best wines are, and always were, quite rare and expensive. Even so, it is still possible to get bargains in Burgundy today.

There are four different sections of Burgundy. To the north is Chablis, celebrated for its crisp, austere white wines. The central and most famous section is the Côte d'Or, composed of the Côte de Nuits to the north and the Côte de Beaune to the south. Central Burgundy includes the Côte Châlonnaise, near the city of Châlon-sur-Saône, and the Mâconnais district, around the city of Mâcon. Finally, in the south, around the city of Lyon there is the Beaujolais, whose inexpensive, quaffable red wine is extremely popular.

The entire province of Burgundy is known as Bourgogne, which is the most general place-name, or appellation contrôlée. Each township in the Côte d'Or is usually coupled with its most famous vineyard, under which its wines may be sold (e.g., Nuits-Saint Georges, Chambolle-Musigny). Within the appellation, there may be individual vineyards that have been legally classified as crus (growths), based on the superior quality of their wine. There are two quality levels: Premiers Crus, or first growths, and Grands Crus, or great growths, rated by

their superior soil and exposure. The best vineyards lie on slopes, at an optimum angle, to assure regular ripening. All but one of the red grands crus are located in the northern Côte de Nuits; the southern Côte de Beaune is primarily noted for its white wines.

Two grape varieties produce the best wines: Pinot Noir for reds, and Chardonnay for whites. Two other grapes are grown in Burgundy: for reds, Gamay, which is used for Beaujolais, and for white, Aligoté. Gamay may sometimes be blended with Pinot Noir to make a wine

called "passe-tout-grains." Aligoté may be grown in secondary vineyards to make a light, easygoing wine called "Bourgogne Aligoté."

Newcomers to Burgundy are often shocked at the high prices, which relates to the small production. By law, vineyards in Burgundy are limited to a maximum of 45 hl/ha (about 475 U.S. gallons/acre). Individual vineyard holdings in Burgundy tend to be small, and shared by several growers. Thus, authentic Burgundy is a scarcity that has never been inexpensive.

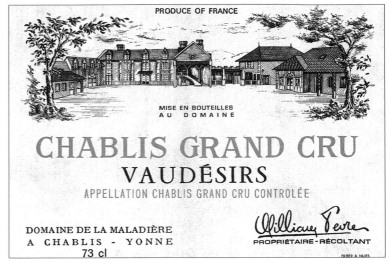

Left: A cluster of very ripe bunches of Pinot Noir at Monthélie, Burgundy.

Below: A cluster of Chardonnay grapes in the Montrachet vineyard, Burgundy, approaching harvest time.

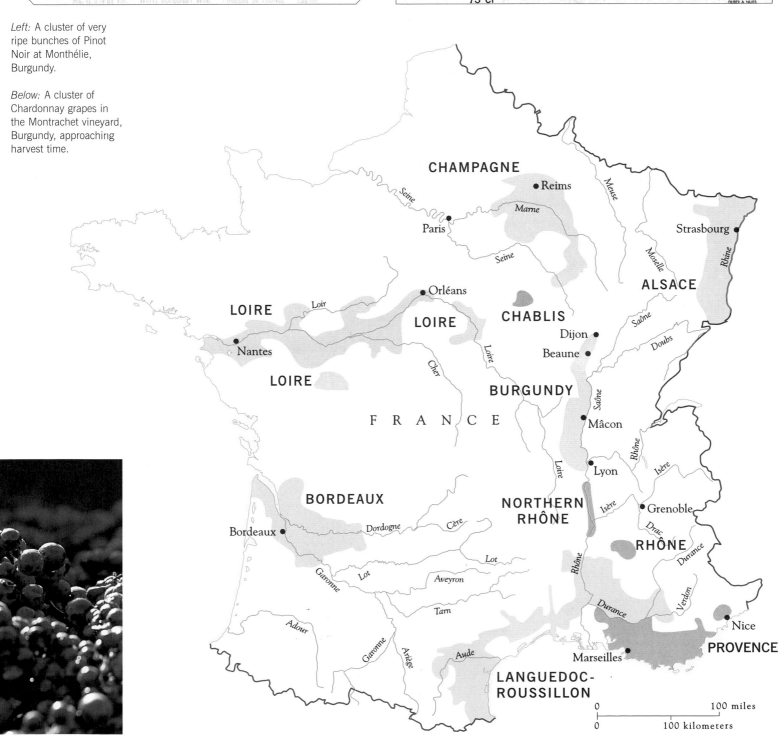

CHAMPAGNE

• Reims

Paris

Strasbourg •

ALSACE

LOIRE

Orléans •

LOIRE

CHABLIS

Dijon •

Beaune •

• Nantes

LOIRE

BURGUNDY

F R A N C E

Mâcon •

Lyon •

BORDEAUX

NORTHERN
RHÔNE

• Grenoble

RHÔNE

Bordeaux •

Nice •

PROVENCE

Marseilles •

LANGUEDOC-
ROUSSILLON

0   100 miles

0   100 kilometers

Burgundy traditionally was marketed by merchants, known as négociants, who bought wine from the growers, blended it to their specifications, and then bottled and shipped it under their own label. Burgundy vintners are now increasingly marketing their wines themselves, under their own label. This practice, known as estate-bottling, is identified by the terms "mis en bouteilles au domaine" (bottled at the domain, estate-bottled) or "mis en bouteilles à la propriété" (bottled at the property).

The following is a roster of Burgundy's best vineyards, listed in overall order of quality, followed by some selected growers and shippers. Do not expect too many bargains – except that by careful selection it is still possible to get good Burgundy for under $10/bottle, even in good vintages.

Chablis

Grand Cru
Les Clos
Grenouilles
Vaudésir
Blanchot
Valmur
Les Preuses
Bougros
La Moutonne

Premier Cru
Fourchaume
Côte de Fontenay
Vaulorent
Fournaux
Montée de Tonnerre
Les Lys
Les Forêts
Monts-de-Milieu
Vaucoupin
Beauroy
Vosgros
Montmains
Mélinots
Butteaux
Séché

Recommended Shippers:

J. Moreau & Co.
Albert Pic
Henri Laroche (Domaine Laroche)
Henri Lamblin
A. Regnard

Recommended Growers:

William Fèvre (Domaine La Maladière)
René Dauvissat
Louis Michel
Robert Vocoret
Simmonet-Febvre
Billaud-Simon

Côte d'Or

In the following table, grands crus appear under their own name, without the name of the informing township. The names of the premiers crus vineyards appear after the township, as they would on a wine label.

Marsannay-la-Côte

Fixin
Fixin Clos de la Perrière
Fixin Clos du Chapitre
Fixin Clos Napoleon

Gevrey-Chambertin
Chambertin
Chambertin Clos de Bèze
Charmes-Chambertin
Latricières-Chambertin
Mazis-Chambertin
Griottes-Chambertin
Ruchottes-Chambertin
Chapelle-Chambertin
Gevrey-Chambertin Clos St. Jacques
Gevrey-Chambertin Lavaux St. Jacques
Gevrey-Chambertin Cazetiers (or Gazetiers)
Gevrey-Chambertin Estournelles
Gevrey-Chambertin Petite Chapelle

Morey-Saint Denis
Clos St. Denis
Bonnes-Mares (part)
Clos des Lambrays
Morey St. Denis Clos des Ormes
Morey St. Denis Clos Bussiere

Chambolle-Musigny
Le Musigny (red & white)
Bonnes-Mares (part)
Chambolle-Musigny Amoureuses
Chambolle-Musigny Charmes

Vougeot
Clos de Vougeot
Vougeot La Perrière

Left: Gevrey-Chambertin, a famous little wine town in the Côte de Nuits, Burgundy.

Right: Jean (right) and Etienne Grivot, a talented father and son team in Vosne-Romanée, who make an excellent Clos de Vougeot.

Below: Nuits-St. Georges, another well-known Burgundy wine town, encircled by famous vineyards.

Flagey-Échezeaux
Grands-Échezeaux
Échezeaux

Vosne-Romanée
Romanée-Conti (monopole), owned by
Domaine de la Romanée-Conti
La Tâche (monopole), owned by
Domaine de la Romanée-Conti
Romanée-Saint Vivant
Richebourg
La Romanée
La Grande Rue
Vosne-Romanée Les Malconsorts
Vosne-Romanée Les Suchots
Vosne-Romanée Les Beaumonts

Nuits-Saint Georges
Les St. Georges
Nuits-St. Georges Les Boudots
Nuits-St. Georges Vaucrains
Nuits-St. Georges Clos des Porrets
Nuits-St. Georges Les Pruliers
Nuits-St. Georges Les Cailles
Nuits-St. Georges Clos de la Maréchale
Nuits-St. Georges Clos des Corvées
Nuits-St. Georges Aux Perdrix
Nuits-St. Georges Les Didiers

Aloxe-Corton
Le Corton (red and white)
Corton-Charlemagne (white only)

Left: Very old bottles at Maison Louis Jadot, in the city of Beaune. Jadot is one of Burgundy's most famous shippers or négociants.

Above: The celebrated Hotel de Dieu, of the Hospices de Beaune, Burgundy, with its dazzling multicolored roof.

Right: Preparing a sample using a "cask thief," or pipette, to draw the wine out of the barrel for appraisal.

Corton-Clos du Roi
Corton-Bressandes
Corton-Renardes
Corton-Pougets
Aloxe-Corton Chaillots

Pernand-Vergelesses
Ile des Vergelesses
Clos de la Croix de Pierre (monopole Louis Jadot)

Savigny-les-Beaune
Savigny-Vergelesses
Savigny-Marconnets
Savigny-Lavières
Savigny-Jarrons
Savigny-Dominode
Savigny Les Guettes
Savigny-Narbantons

Chorey-les-Beaune
Beaune
Beaune Fèves
Beaune Grèves
Beaune Clos du Roi
Beaune Clos de la Vigne au Saint
Beaune Marconnets
Beaune Clos des Mouches

Pommard
Pommard Épenots
Pommard Rugiens

Left: A Burgundy producer shows wines to a visiting buyer.

Below: Monsieur Parent, of the famous Burgundy domaine, pouring glasses for his guests. Thomas Jefferson was one of the estate's first US customers.

Right: Forgoing the customary Tastevin and designer stemware, this Burgundian seems to be properly engaged in his work.

Pommard Clos de la Commaraine
Pommard Clos Blanc
Pommard Les Arvelets
Pommard Pézerolles
Pommard Les Jarollières

Volnay
Volnay Caillerets
Volnay Champans
Volnay Frémiets
Volnay Clos des Ducs
Volnay Santenots
Volnay Clos des Chênes
Volnay Mitans

Auxey-Duresses
Auxey-Duresses Les Duresses
Auxey-Duresses Le Val
Auxey-Duresses Reugné

Meursault
Meursault-Perrières
Meursault Clos des Perrières
Meursault-Genevrières
Meursault-Goutte d'Or
Meursault-Charmes
Meursault-Poruzots
Meursault-Jennelotte
Meursault-La Pièce sous le Bois
Meursault-Dos d'Ane

Puligny-Montrachet
Le Montrachet (part)
Chevalier-Montrachet

Bâtard-Montrachet
Bienvenue-Bâtard-Montrachet
Puligny-Montrachet Combettes
Puligny-Montrachet Pucelles
Puligny-Montrachet Caillerets
Puligny-Montrachet Clavoillon
Puligny-Montrachet Réferts
Puligny-Montrachet Les Chalumeaux
Puligny-Montrachet Perrières

Chassagne-Montrachet
Le Montrachet (part)
Criots-Bâtard-Montrachet
Chassagne-Montrachet Ruchottes
Chassagne-Montrachet Morgeot
Chassagne-Montrachet Clos St. Jean
Chassagne-Montrachet La Boudriotte

Saint-Aubin

Santenay
Santenay Gravières
Santenay Clos Rousseau
Santenay La Comme
Santenay Beauregard
Santenay La Maladière

Growers and shippers may sell blends of wines from different townships as "Côte de Nuits-Villages" or "Côte de Beaune-Villages," if it is a blend of at least two different townships in either section. The most basic wines may be sold as simply "Bourgogne rouge" (red) or

"Bourgogne blanc" (white), which have lower minimum quality standards. An older low-ranking appellation, Bourgogne Ordinaire or Bourgogne Grande Ordinaire, is risky and rarely seen nowadays.

The Burgundy wine trade revolves around the city of Beaune, and the largest shippers or négociants have their headquarters there. Despite an old reputation for excessive blending, most négociants today usually make reliable, well-structured Burgundies. The only catch is

that a high price does not always represent a guarantee of quality – even with some of the leading producers in the area.

Recommended Négociants:

Joseph Drouhin
Louis Jadot
Louis Latour
Domaine Leroy
Bouchard Père et Fils
Bouchard Ainé et Fils (not presently sold in USA)
Remoissenet Père & Fils
Maison Jaffelin
Domaine Faiveley
Maison Ropiteau (Domaine Ropiteau-Mignon for estate wines)
Labouré-Roi
Coron Père & Fils
Albert Bichot
Chartron & Trebuchet
Olivier Leflaive
Pierre Ponnelle
Chanson
Jean-Claude Boisset

Recommended Growers

(arranged geographically, north to south)
Armand Rousseau
Pierre Gelin
Clair-Daü
Domaine Méo-Camuzet
Domaine Drouhin-Laroze
Domaine Trapet
Domaine Dujac
Domaine Jean-Marie Ponsot
Domaine Roumier
Domaine Lignier
Comte de Voguë
Jean Grivot
L'Heritier-Guyot
Domaine de la Romanée-Conti
Domaine Jean & Michel Gros
René Engel
Henri Lamarche
Domaine Mongeard-Mugneret
Domaine Henri Jayer
Domaine Henri Gouges
Domaine Chantal Lescure
Domaine Rapet
Domaine Bonneau de Martray
Domaine Chandon de Briailles
Domaine Simon Bize et Fils
Prince Florent de Mérode
Domaine Tollot-Beaut
Hospices de Beaune

Below: Red wines of the Hospices de Beaune are always a treat to taste, even more so with a baguette of bread and some local cheese.

Below right: Pichon-Longueville-Baron, one of the most famous estates in Pauillac, is now the property of the AXA insurance group.

Domaine Duchet
Comte Armand
Domaine Parent
Domaine de Courcel
Marquis d'Angerville, Volnay
Domaine Henri Boillot
Domaine Clerget
Château de Pommard
Domaine Jean-Claude Monnier
Comte Lafon, Meursault
Domaine Henri Clerc
Domaine Patrick Javillier
Domaine Grivault
Domaine Étienne Sauzet
Domaine Leflaive
Domaine Coche-Dury
Domaine Gaunoux
Domaine Bernard Morey
Domaine Jacques Morey
Domaine Marc Morey
Domaine Jean-Noel Gagnard
Domaine Colin

Côte Châlonnaise

The Côte d'Or essentially ends at Sante-nay, but Burgundy's vineyards continue south into the Côte Châlonnaise, where soil and climate is favorable to Pinot Noir and Chardonnay. Although vineyards here do not enjoy quite the same ideal soil and exposure as in the Côte d'Or, many excellent wines are grown – and many are still relatively inexpensive.

The two chief wine-growing town-ships are Mercurey and Rully, respectively famous for their reds and whites; recently many growers have planted more Chardonnay in Mercurey's vineyards, in response to strong demand. The wines are generous and smooth, and are still not too expensive. There are two other towns on the Côte Châlonnaise: Givry, noted mainly for its reds; and Montagny, the most southerly, which makes exclusively white wines. A few négociants from the Côte d'Or have recently supplemented their offerings with wines from these areas. The following is a list of vineyards:

Mercurey
Clos des Myglands
Clos du Roy
Clos Jacquelet
Clos Rochettes

Givry
Clos St. Pierre
Clos St. Paul
La Baraude
Clos Salomon
Servois
Clos des Moines

Rully
Montagny
Les Charmelottes
Vignes du Soleil
Les Bonnevaux
Sous Les Roches
Les Chanteoiseaux

Mâconnais

Most of what is called "white Burgundy" would not exist if it were not for the Mâconnais, an important growing area surrounding the city of Mâcon. Here Chardonnay is king. Growing conditions in the Mâconnais are ideal for white wines. Vineyards here tend to be more productive than they are further north. The most basic appellation is Mâcon, either as red (rouge) or white (blanc), which is produced anywhere in the Mâconnais area: Red Mâcon is seldom seen, eclipsed in popularity by the superior whites. "Mâcon" or "Mâcon Supérieur" indicates that the wine was made only within the township of the city of Mâcon; the word Mâcon, followed by the name of a township or village, indicates that the wine was produced only in that area. These are the popular "Mâcon-Villages," which are either sold

under this name or a more specific indication of origin, such as Mâcon-Lugny, Mâcon-Viré or Mâcon-Fuissé.

North of Mâcon itself, there are several vineyard sites that bear their own appellations. The most famous of these is Pouilly-Fuissé, a popular white Burgundy; there are a few single-vineyard Pouilly-Fuissés, but most of what is sold is blended and bottled by shippers, without any further indication of vineyard. Two nearby appellations, Pouilly-Vinzelles and Pouilly-Loché, named for the townships in which they are located, are lighter than Pouilly-Fuissé, but are often good substitutes.

Perhaps the best value in the entire area is Saint-Véran. The region essentially surrounds the Pouilly-Fuissé area, and is composed of eight townships north and south of Fuissé and Chaintré that have similar growing conditions. Saint-Vérans can often approach a good Pouilly-Fuissé for a lot less money.

Beaujolais

Grown in an extensive area that begins south of the city of Mâcon and leads all the way down to Lyon, Beaujolais is Burgundy's most productive wine region. In addition to being relatively inexpensive and straightforward, Beaujolais involves different production techniques than are used in the Côte d'Or and the Mâconnais districts. Beaujolais can be either a red wine, produced from Gamay; or it may be a white wine, made from Chardonnay and sold as Beaujolais blanc. The flavor of Gamay in the Beaujolais wines is fresh and fruity. The wines drink well during their first year, rarely improving with bottle age.

Normal red winemaking in Burgundy involves a regular crushing of the grapes, followed by extended skin contact or cuvaison. In Beaujolais the growers use a different method, known as carbonic maceration. At harvest time, grapes are

Left: At Arcachon, on the bay, a plate of oysters is perfectly enhanced with a white Bordeaux.

Right: Château Margaux, a notable first growth Bordeaux estate, with its elegant columns at the main entrance. Since the 1980s it has become one of the most successful Médocs.

Chiroubles (very light, usually best in their first year)
Regnié (new appellation – usually rather light)
Brouilly (lively and zesty)
Côte de Brouilly (sturdier)
Saint-Amour
Fleurie (fine fruit; a very popular Beaujolais)
Juliénas (a bit obscure, for this reason often a good buy)
Chénas
Morgon (usually better in its 2nd year)
Moulin-à-Vent (generally the richest, finest and most costly)

Individual vineyard Beaujolais are relatively rare. The style and quality standards of the shipper are usually more important than a specific vineyard site. For this reason I recommend the following shippers, who specialize in better wines from the Beaujolais area:

Georges Duboeuf
Paul Beaudet
Louis Tête
Trénel & Fils
Jean Bedin
Jean-Marc Aujoux
Colin & Borisset
Sylvain Fessy
Robert Sarrau

❀ Bordeaux ❀

Bordeaux is France's southwestern capital of wine-growing. No other major wine district has so much land entitled to appellation contrôlée vineyards (350,000 acres); for this reason, and also because of the long heritage of wine-growing in Bordeaux, the name has become synonymous with the best in French wine.

Bordeaux's potential largely relates to its soil and its location. From its position along the Gironde, an estuary that leads to the Atlantic, Bordeaux was ideally suited to supply wine traders all over western Europe. Most of Bordeaux's vineyards are laid out by the system of châteaux, or castles, some of which date back to the middle ages. Wines bottled at the estate or château bear the designation "mis en bouteilles au château," which legally means the same thing as estate-bottling. Because the grape grower

brought to the winery and placed in a sealed tank, uncrushed, where they remain for about a week. The gentle weight of the grapes is enough to crush them slightly, and fermentation takes place on its own, without any exposure to air. After a week, the grapes are pressed and the wine ferments out to dryness.

Carbonic maceration gives Beaujolais much of its unique fruity character. The process dates back only some three decades; for years, it was popular in restaurants in Paris and Lyon to drink the new wine within weeks after it was made – the so-called "vin nouveau," or "vin de l'année." Beginning in the early 1970s, a few Beaujolais producers began shipping

Beaujolais Nouveau to world markets, after the fifteenth of November. Soon a large portion of the annual harvest was sold as Beaujolais Nouveau (or its alternate term, Beaujolais Primeur). Beaujolais Nouveau is still a seasonal delight, and many producers offer this light and fruity red wine.

There are a few townships in Beaujolais-Villages that sell wine under their own name: these are the so-called cru Beaujolais, which more closely resemble wines from the Côte d'Or even though they are produced from Gamay. To identify the styles of the cru Beaujolais, I have grouped the wines in terms of their usual strength, lightest wines first:

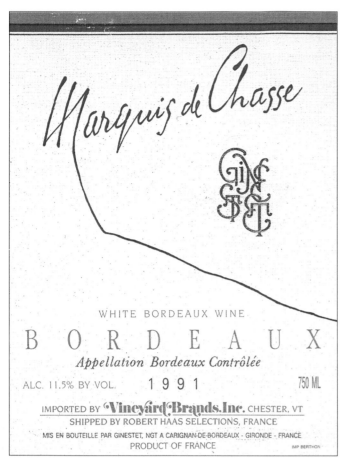

Right: The entrance to Château Lafite-Rothschild in Pauillac.

is also the winemaker, thus exercising more control throughout all the steps of wine-growing, a château-bottled Bordeaux is your guarantee of authenticity.

But not all good Bordeaux has to be château-bottled. Owing to the region's size, there is a wealth of good wine available for blending into well-known brands or marques, and depending on the vintage and the shipper's standards, some of them can be very good indeed. Also, in certain areas there are cooperative cellars, or caves coopératives, that buy grapes under contract from growers who belong to the cooperative. You should also consider these popular branded Bordeaux, which have been consistently good in recent vintages: Mouton-Cadet (Domaine Rothschild), La Cour-Pavillon, Grande Marque, Barton & Guestier, Marquis de Chasse, Verdillac.

Wine produced in the delimited area of Bordeaux is entitled to the appellation Bordeaux; if it is at least 1% alcohol above the minimum, it may be sold as Bordeaux Supérieur. The appellation describes red, white and rosé wines from approved varieties; sparkling wines are also produced, though they are less widely seen. Ironically, although Bor-

deaux's traditional fame relates to its fine red wines, commonly known as "clarets," the region as a whole grows more white wine than red.

The principal wine regions in Bordeaux are the Médoc, Graves, Sauternes and Barsac (which are a part of Graves), Premières Côtes de Bordeaux, Entre-Deux-Mers, Pomerol, Saint-Emilion, Côtes de Castillon, Fronsac, Canon-Fronsac, Côtes de Bourg and Premières Côtes de Blaye. In each of these districts there may be individual parishes that collectively form a part of the growing area, in which case the best wines will qualify for a more specific appellation. The smallest land parcels, and usually the best, are the châteaux themselves. Their wines are famous throughout the world, and they can be counted on to provide superb wines in most vintages.

Many grapes thrive in Bordeaux's sunny climate, but only a few give the best results. Bordeaux growers have learned to rely on a blend of different varieties, not just a single grape. Experience shows that a mix of different grapes, planted according to soil and location, gives the best wine. The chief red grape is Cabernet Sauvignon, a reliable, pro-

ductive grape that may be easily grown on a wide variety of soils. A related variety is Cabernet Franc, which gives good but more straightforward wines. For added complexity and softness, they may be supplanted with Merlot, which gives lovely fruit and scent; in the Médoc Petit-Verdot, a rich supplemental variety, is also grown.

No less important are Bordeaux's white varieties. The principal white grape is Sauvignon Blanc, related to Cabernet Sauvignon and grown in many other parts of France. Wines made from Sauvignon Blanc typically have a light, pleasant herbaceous flavor; they may be grown entirely from the varietal, or blended with the rounder, fruitier Sémillon. It is important to differentiate three distinct types of Bordeaux whites.

The first style is a light, crisp dry white destined to be drunk in its first or second year. These "new wave" white Bordeaux are produced essentially from Sauvignon Blanc. Rising demand for this type of wine prompted Bordeaux growers to plant Sauvignon Blanc in areas where red grapes were formerly grown. A good example of this type of wine can be found in Entre-Deux-Mers, whose lively, fresh

WINESHARE

Certificate of Registration
to a 'row' of 50 vines
Row No ?????, at
Château de Pizay

Given to:

Your Choice of Words Here

....

....

Presented by:

Your Choice of Words

....

....

A humourous/serious/sentimental message, dates, occasions etc
Call us if you need any help

....

....

Signed on behalf of WineShare

white wines usually represent outstanding bargains.

A second type of white Bordeaux is best exemplified by the dependable white Graves often seen on restaurant wine lists. As opposed to the lively first style, which should be drunk very young, these wines have more Sémillon in the blend, and improve with some time in bottle.

There is a third type of Bordeaux white that is possible in only a few of the world's vineyards. Late harvesting is a technique practiced in a few celebrated wine districts. In the Sauternes and Barsac areas, the Sémillon and Sauvi-gnon Blanc grapes frequently become overripe, and are subject to the action of a special, beneficial mold, Botrytis cinerea. Grapes are then harvested individually. But the right conditions for sweet wines do not occur each vintage, and even in a good vintage a Sauternes château might only produce about 20% of a comparable red wine estate in Bordeaux. So the wines do not come cheap. Less expensive substitutes may be found in the adjoining Cérons, Cadillac, Loupiac and Sainte-Croix-du-Mont areas, where there is a long tradition of sweet white wine production.

The Médoc

The Médoc begins just north of the city of Bordeaux, and continues along the eastern flank of a broad peninsula towards the mouth of the Gironde. Because of its ideal location, excellent soils and consistent weather, the Médoc stands as one of France's foremost wine regions. The central section is known as Haut-Médoc, and while each of its communes is planted principally in Cabernet Sauvignon, the proportion of Merlot and Cabernet Franc changes in each vineyard – and in some even a little Petit-Verdot is

grown. The following characteristics apply to each commune.

Margaux, the first major township to the south, produces soft, medium-bodied wines with great scent and elegance. Saint-Julien, some distance to the north, tends to have a bit more depth. Pauillac, the largest commune, has many of the most famous châteaux. Finally Saint-Estèphe, to the north, typically grows rugged red wines which are a treat for the collector with patience. In addition, there are some other townships outside of these areas that can only sell wines as Haut-Médoc: Ludon, Listrac, Moulis, Lamarque, and Saint-Laurent. Estates in these areas cannot demand the same high prices, and recently their wines have surged ahead in quality.

In 1855, in preparation for a Paris exposition that same year, the most famous Bordeaux châteaux were officially classified according to quality – each château in the 1855 classification was designated as a cru, or growth, in five different categories, based on the price. While this was a major step for the Bordeaux wine trade, it did have several shortcomings. Only the Médoc estates, plus one red Graves, were classified, along with Sauternes and Barsac. Price was the original factor for selection, but prices have of course since changed. Finally, the 1855 classification describes only a small portion of all the wine grown in Bordeaux. But with only one exception, the 1855 classification has not changed for over a century, and it should remain well into the next century.

Left: Anthony Barton, the proprietor of Château Léoville-Barton in Saint-Julien.

Right: Château Léoville-Barton in the Médoc.

Hundreds of other wine estates lie throughout the Médoc, which are either located outside the primary communes or whose estates were not classified in 1855. Officially these fall into three categories: "crus exceptionnels," or exceptional growths, and "crus bourgeois" or middle growths, which has an additional and somewhat confusing quality category of "crus bourgeois supérieur." These are popular, often outstanding wines produced by estates that could well be included in a new Bordeaux classification. The better estates are as follows (Estates in italics are especially recommended):

crus exceptionnels
Villegeorge
Lanessan
Angludet
Chasse-Spleen
Poujeaux-Theil
La Couronne
Moulin-Riche
Bel Air-Marquis d'Aligre

crus bourgeois
Meyney
Phélan-Ségur
de Pez
Les Ormes-de-Pez
Haut-Marbuzet
Marbuzet
Cordeillan-Bages
Gloria
du Glana
Larose-Trintaudon
Terrey-Gros-Cailloux
Tronquoy-Lalande

Moulis
Branas-Grand-Poujeaux
Brillette
Dutruch-Grand-Poujeaux
Gressier-Grand-Poujeaux
Maucaillou
Poujeaux

Listrac
La Bécade
Clarke (Rothschild)
Deyrem-Valentin

Fonréaud
Fourcas-Dupré
Fourcas-Hosten
Lafon
La Tour-du-Haut-Moulin
Lestage
Lamarque
Malescasse
Marsac-Seguineau
La Tour-de-Mons
Sénéjac
Sociando-Mallet

Beginning in the 1960s, certain top Médoc châteaux began releasing a second wine, made from younger vines or vats that were not considered worthy of the main label. This practice became widespread in the last decade, and depending on the estate in question, their second wine can be much like the main label, for a lot less money. In the following list of classified growths, where applicable, the second wine is listed next to the first. The 1855 classification of the Médoc (1996 status):

First growths
Lafite-Rothschild

Latour
Margaux

Haut-Brion
Mouton-Rothschild

Second growths
Rausan-Ségla
Rauzan-Gassies

Leoville-Las-Cases
Leoville-Barton
Leoville-Poyferré
Durfort-Vivens

Gruaud-Larose
Lascombes
*Pichon-Longueville
-Baron*
Pichon-Longueville,
Comtesse de Lalande

Brane-Cantenac
Ducru-Beaucaillou

Second wine
*Carruades de
Château Lafite-
Rothschild*
Les Forts de Latour
*Pavillon Rouge du
Château Margaux*
Bahans-Haut-Brion
*Deuxieme Vin de
Mouton-Rothschild*

Enclos de
Moncabon
Clos du Marquis

Moulin-Riche
Domaine de Cure-
Bourse
Larose-Sarget
Segonnes
Réserve du Baron

Reserve de la
Comtesse de "L"
Notton
Clos la Croix

Cos d'Estournel

Montrose

Third growths
Kirwan
d'Issan
Lagrange
Langoa-Barton
Giscours
Malescot-St. Exupéry
Cantenac-Brown
Boyd-Cantenac
Palmer
La Lagune

Desmirail
Calon-Ségur
Ferrière
Marquis d'Alesme
Becker

Fourth growths
Saint-Pierre
Talbot
Branaire-Ducru
*Duhart-Milon-
Rothschild*

Château du
Marbuzet
La Dame de
Montrose

"private reserve"

Les Fiefs de Lagrange
Lady Langoa

Reserve du Général
Ludon-Pomys-
Agassac
Baudry
Marquis de Ségur

Connétable Talbot

Moulin de Duhart

Above left: Château Cos d'Estournel, a landmark in the St. Estèphe area, greets you as you drive north on route D2.

Below left: Château Cantenac-Brown, in the township of Margaux, as seen from the air.

Above: Château Beychevelle, in St. Julien, is celebrated for its beautiful landscaping and statues.

GRAND VIN DE BORDEAUX
DOMAINE DE CHEVALIER
SPECIMEN
GRAND CRU CLASSE
1978
GRAVES   75 cl
APPELLATION GRAVES CONTROLÉE
JEAN RICARD PROPRIÉTAIRE A LÉOGNAN (GIRONDE) FRANCE
MIS EN BOUTEILLE AU CHATEAU
PRODUCE OF FRANCE

BORDEAUX
GRAND CRU CLASSÉ
CHATEAU PAPE CLÉMENT
APPELLATION GRAVES CONTROLÉE
1961
Ste MONTAGNE & Cie PROPRIÉTAIRE A PESSAC-GIRONDE
MIS EN BOUTEILLE AU CHATEAU
DÉPOSÉ

1975
CHATEAU HAUT-BERGEY
Léognan

CRU DE GRAVES
Appellation Graves Contrôlée
✿
J. DESCHAMPS
PROPRIÉTAIRE A LÉOGNAN (GIRONDE)
• • •

Pouget
La Tour-Carnet   Sire de Camin
Lafon-Rochet
Beychevelle   *Reserve L'Amiral*
Prieuré-Lichine   Clairefont
Marquis de Terme   Les Gondats

Fifth growths
Pontet-Canet   *Les Hauts de Pontet*
Batailley
Haut-Batailley   *La Tour l'Aspic*
Grand-Puy-Lacoste   Lacoste-Borie
Grand-Puy-Ducasse   Artigues-Arnaud
Lynch-Bages   Haut Bages-
    Avérous
Lynch-Moussas
Dauzac
Mouton d'Armailhac
du Tertre
Haut Bages-Libéral
Pédésclaux   Bellerose
Belgrave
Camensac
Cos Labory
Clerc-Milon-Rothschild

Croizet-Bages
Cantemerle

Graves
Haut-Brion (also in 1855 classification)
La Mission-Haut-Brion
La Tour Haut-Brion
Laville-Haut-Brion
Pape-Clément
Couhins
Couhins-Lurton
Domaine de Chevalier
Haut-Bailly   Domaine de la
    Parde
Carbonnieux
Fieuzal
La Tour-Martillac
Malartic-Lagravière
Olivier
Smith-Haut-Lafitte
Bouscaut   Valoux

Not all Graves has to be classified to be good. Among many estates, here are some recommendations:

Above: Jean-Michel Cazes, proprietor of Château Lynch-Bages and Les Ormes-de-Pez, is a central personality in the Médoc.

Left: Roses are popular in many Bordeaux vineyards. These adorn vines in Sauternes.

Above right: Château Raymond-Lafon, in the heart of the Sauternes area, with its formal gardens.

Baret
Les Carmes-Haut-Brion
Chantegrive (other labels: Bon Dieu-des-Vignes, Mayne-Leveque)
Cruzeau
Graville-Lacoste
Haut-Bergey
La Louvière
Larrivet-Haut-Brion
Magence
Le Pape
Picque-Caillou
des Portets (Graves/Portets)
Rahoul
Respide-Médeville
Roquetaillade-La-Grange
St. Pierre
Toumilon
Tourteau-Chollet

Sauternes
Grand Premier Cru
d'Yquem

Premiers Crus
La Tour-Blanche
Lafaurie-Peyraguey
Clos Haut-Peyraguey
Rayne-Vigneau
Suduiraut
Coutet
Climens
Guiraud
Rieussec
Rabaud-Promis
Sigalas-Rabaud

Deuxièmes Crus
Myrat
Doisy-Daëne
Doisy-Dubroca
Doisy-Vedrines
d'Arche
Filhot
Broustet
Nairac
Caillou

Suau
de Malle
Romer-du-Hayot
Lamothe
Lamothe-Guignard

In addition to the classed estates, there are several others that are worth mentioning: Bastor-Lamontagne, de Fargues (owned by Lur-Saluces of Yquem), Gilette & Les Justices (Médéville), Raymond-Lafon, and Rolland.

Saint-Emilion

A major shortcoming with the 1855 classification was resolved in 1955, when the vineyards of Saint-Emilion finally received their due. Three groups were used, according the traditionally famous estates the rank of "Premier Grand Cru Classé," first great growths, followed by a larger set of Grands Crus Classés. Below

Left: Madame Bechon, tending to some young vines at Château Cheval Blanc. This work is called cavaillon.

Below: Château Bastor-Lamontagne, a notable estate in the Sauternes region, recently very celebrated for its wines.

Right: Hubert de Bouard, proprietor of Château l'Angelus in St. Emilion, obviously very proud of his estate which was recently promoted to a premier grand cru classé.

this rank, there is the plain Saint-Emilion Grand Cru, or, for the most basic wines, Saint-Emilion. Because most estates qualify, the system in Saint-Emilion was much more democratic.

Unlike those of the Médoc, which rely predominantly on Cabernet Sauvignon, Saint-Emilions are made mostly from Merlot, with a little Cabernet Franc for complexity. They typically have plenty of scent and generosity, and there is much to choose from.

The classified properties in Saint-Emilion tend to be small. Wines from this list, therefore, are usually fairly expensive, even in less successful vintages. But because of the region's high quality standards, you will usually be well rewarded when you order a good Saint-Emilion. The 1955 classification of Saint-Emilion (1996 status):

Premier Grand Cru Classé: "A"
Ausone
Cheval-Blanc

Premier Grand Cru Classé: "B"
L'Angelus
Belair

Beauséjour-Bécot
Beauséjour-Duffau-Lagarosse
Canon
Clos Fourtet
Figeac
La Gaffelière
Magdelaine
Pavie
Trottevieille

Grand Cru Classé
L'Arrosée
Baleau
Balestard-La Tonnelle
Bellevue

Bergat
Berliquet
Cadet-Piola
Canon-La Gaffelière
Capdemourlin
Chapelle-Madeleine
Chauvin
Clos des Jacobins
Corbin
Corbin-Michotte
Couvent des Jacobins
Croque-Michotte
Curé-Bon La Madelaine
Dassault
Faurie-de-Souchard

Fonplégade
Fonroque
Franc-Mayne
Grand-Barrail-Lamarzelle-Figeac
Grand Corbin
Grand Corbin-Despagne
Grand-Mayne
Grand Pontet
Guadet-Saint-Julien
Haut-Corbin
Haut-Sarpe
La Carte
La Clotte
La Clusière
La Dominique
La Madeleine
Lamarzelle

Larmande
Laniote
Larcisse-Ducasse
Laroze
La Serre
La Tour-du-Pin-Figeac (Bélivier)
La Tour-du-Pin-Figeac (Moueix)
Matras
Mauvezin
Moulin-de-Cadet
Clos L'Oratoire
Pavie-Decesse
Pavie-Macquin
Pavillon-Cadet
Petit-Faurie-de-Soutard
Le Prieuré
Ripeau
St. Georges-Côte-Pavie
Clos Saint-Martin
Sansonnet
Soutard
Tertre-Daügay
Tour-Figeac
Trimoulet
Trois-Moulins
Troplong-Mondot
Villemaurine
Yon-Figeac

In addition, Saint-Emilion has some outlying villages around the town itself that add their name when selling their wines. The best known include Saint-Georges-St. Emilion, Montagne-St. Emilion, Lussac-St. Emilion, and Sables-St. Emilion. Their wines are correspond-

ingly less expensive and many are excellent: Saint-Georges, Monbousquet, Vieux Château Guibeau, Fombrauge, Toinet-Fombrauge, Calon, Belair-Montaiguillon, Plaisance, Patris, La Pelleterie.

Pomerol

The rich, supple wines of Pomerol are, at their best, silky smooth and make a profound statement about Merlot. But while the best Saint-Emilion estates tend to be small, those in Pomerol are even smaller. The entire region under vines is barely 1,000 acres, so do not expect too many bargains.

Pomerol has no official classification. Even the humblest estates can be expensive, owing to their scarcity. In addition, there is the adjacent area of Lalande-de-Pomerol, where many of the wines are not well-known and some can be excellent. What follows is an annotated list of leading Pomerol estates, based on their general reputation. There is one single outstanding Pomerol, Château Pétrus, managed by Jean-Pierre Moueix, that is among the rarest and most expensive of all Bordeaux wines. Other top estates include:

Vieux-Château-Certan
Lafleur
L'Evangile
La Conseillante
Trotanoy

Lafleur-Pétrus
Beauregard
Le Pin
Bon Pasteur
Certan-de-May
Clinet
Clos l'Eglise
La Croix
La Croix-de-Gay
Feytit-Clinet
Le Gay
Gazin
La Grave de Pomerol (Moueix)
L'Eglise-Clinet
Moulinet
Nenin
Plince
La Pointe
Clos René
Rouget
de Sales
La Violette

Fronsac

Fronsac is an old wine district with a great heritage of rich, long-lasting wines. Fronsacs remained obscure for many years and were unfamiliar to most wine drinkers outside France. Now the area,

Left: Tying up or training the vines (remontage) at Château Barbe Blanche, Lussac-St. Emilion.

Below: Château de Sales, Pomerol, one of the larger estates in the area.

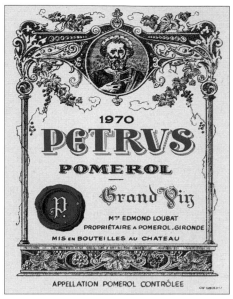

made up of Fronsac and Canon-Fronsac, is in a renaissance and some of the estates are staging a brilliant comeback. Here are the principal estates:

Canon
Canon-de-Brem
La Daüphine
Junayme
La Rivière
Rouet
La Duchesse

La Vieille Cure
Toumalin
Moulin-Haut-Villars
de Carles

Côtes du Castillon

England's rule of Aquitaine ended on the fields of Castillon in 1453, and the town is appropriately known as Castillon-la-Bataille. The vineyards lie to the east of Saint-Emilion, and while the wines tend to be lighter, they share some similarities. Merlot and Cabernet Franc are the dominant grapes here, and the following estates may be counted on to give good results:

Pitray
Tour-Bigorre
Paret-Beauséjour
Faugère
Moulin-Rouge
Lartigue

Bourg and Blaye

The so-called "right bank" of the Gironde has plenty of potential, including acres of vineyard not actually in production; and although some wines are inconsistent, the area overall is a sleeping giant. The wines tend to be soft and supple, similar to those of St. Emilion; the varietal mixture is more apt to be Merlot and Cabernet Franc, rather than Cabernet Sauvignon. Côtes de Bourg reds have plenty of appeal. The better estates include:

de Barbe
Caruel
Civrac
Falfas
de la Grave
Laurensanne
La Grolet
La Croix-Millorit
Le Piat
Rousset
Tayac
Tour-Séguy

❋ Champagne ❋

The wine of choice for toasts and celebrations, Champagne is one of the world's most festive beverages and is relatively rare despite its great fame. It is grown in a delimited area some 150 km (90 miles) east of Paris, where the right combination of climate, location and special chalk soil converges to create a special growing area for sparkling wine production.

It should first be pointed out that the name Champagne refers to a wine, the informing region, and the process by which the wine is made. So much sparkling wine around the world is sold as "champagne" that the word has become synonymous with sparkling wine itself; properly, however, Champagne when capitalized defines only a wine from that region in France. While virtually any wine region can produce a respectable sparkling wine, the Champagne district wants to protect its producers, who use a long, intensive process that they call the méthode champenoise, or Champagne method.

The Champagne region originally began by making still wines, but over the centuries the growers discovered that the wines had a tendency to re-ferment during the winter and become sparkling. This came about when wines were sealed in bottle, and then in the spring, when temperatures gradually rose, a second fermentation would take place. The challenge faced by the growers was to tame this phenomenon, and make a sparkling wine without exploding the container in which it was placed. The methods used to achieve this goal were perfected over several centuries, with the result that Champagne as we now know it is only about 200 years old.

The Champagne district is the most northerly wine region in France. The region is cool, the growing season is short, and is often hindered by unpredictable weather: hail and frost are common. However, these natural hardships are ideal for high acidity in grapes that is ideal for sparkling wine. Three grape varieties are used in making Champagne.

The most widely planted is Pinot Noir, a black grape well suited to the cool climate. At harvest time the juice is extracted away from the skins, so that no color is extracted. Similar results are obtained from Pinot Meunier. The finest and most delicate Champagnes come from Chardonnay, grown in the southern part of the region; the fame of these wines led to the term "blanc de blancs," meaning a white wine made from only white grapes.

Vineyards in Champagne are located in three principal areas: 1) the Montagne de Reims, a rugged plateau north of the city of Reims, yielding fine, classic, full-bodied wines; 2) the Vallée de la Marne, west of Reims along the Marne River Valley, consisting of sloping vineyards that have different soil and exposure and tend to produce softer, more subtle wines; and 3) the Côte des Blancs, the most southerly district, a chalk outcropping located just above the city of Epernay and almost exclusively planted in white Chardonnay grapes. The Champagne district has been ranked by the system of cru (growth), according to the

Left: Chalk formation in the Champagne district – a graphic description of how chalky soil and fine wine go hand in hand.

Above: Abbey de Hautvillers in the heart of the Champagne region.

Right: Taittinger's vineyards at La Marquetterie, Epernay, during the flowering or fleuraison.

Left: Bottles at Maison Ruinart, Reims, Champagne. These bottles have been disgorged and are awaiting final labeling for shipment

Above: Harvest scene in Champagne. Usually the picking is carried out in rather chilly conditions, so these workers come prepared for all types of weather.

Right: Headquarters of Maison Bollinger, Champagne, in the town of Ay.

potential of each township: only hillsides with a soil rich in chalk may be planted in vineyards.

Only a few vineyards in Champagne produce wines exclusively from one vineyard. Virtually all of the wine sold is a blend of wines from many different locations, selected by the producer for a number of different quality traits. Each firm has its own individual style and quality standards, reflected not only in the price of the wine produced but in its character: some Champagnes are fuller and fruitier, while others are more subtle and delicate.

The first steps in Champagne production begin just before the harvest, when a committee of growers, shippers and regional professionals decides on the price to be paid for a kilo of grapes, based on market conditions, cellar stocks from previous vintages, and the expected yield of the vintage. When the grapes are harvested, they are crushed by special calibrated presses that initially release only a small amount of juice from the first pressing. This first, high-quality juice is known as the vin de cuvée. The grapes may be

Left: The essential process of preparing the cuvée, or blend, to determine the house style of a Champagne.

Below: The press house (vendangeoir) used by Maison Veuve Clicquot, in the village of Bouzy. Many of the Champagne firms have these facilities all over the region.

Right: Riddling bottles at Maison Pol Roger, in Epernay, one of the more traditional firms in the district.

Below right: La Marquetterie in Epernay, property of Champagne Taittinger, is used for receptions.

pressed further to yield more juice, but since it has more tannins and extracts from the grapes and stalks, this juice does not go into the best Champagne and is used for other wines, such as the Côteaux Champenois – still white wines from the Champagne district.

After the first fermentation, wines from a number of different sources are brought into each firm, and are tasted and compared by a team of skilled tasters. This careful selection is known as the process of cuvée. Over a period of several weeks, these tasters will decide which wines will go into the final blend preferred by the firm, and whether or not a portion of the wines will be good enough to be sold as a vintage. This last consideration is very important: most Champagne is a blend of different years and is not sold as a vintage, whereas in some years the quality of the crop is high enough to warrant the best lots being sold as a single vintage year. Theoretically, because the base lots are superior, a vintage Champagne is finer than a non-vintage, but as it is rarer and more costly,

the differences are relatively minor to most wine drinkers.

Once the base wines are selected, they are prepared to be made sparkling. A carefully measured mixture of sugar and yeast (known as the liqueur de tirage, or bottling dosage) is introduced in each bottle, and the wines are allowed

to rest over a period of several months. During this time, the wines will become sparkling, but yeast remainders will settle on the bottom of the bottle and have to be removed. Madame Veuve Clicquot-Ponsardin, scion of the famous firm that bears her name, developed the technique of remuage, or riddling (mentioned ear-

CHAMPAGNE

Veuve Clicquot Ponsardin

VENDANGEOIR

lier). After the dégorgement, or disgorging of the yeast remainders, the wine is now ready to be sold, but before it is sealed for good, the wine is given a "shipping dosage," (a mixture of sugar syrup and wine) known as the liqueur d'expédition, in preparation for the market where it will be sold.

At this stage, the wine is austerely dry; a specific category has been established in Champagne for grades of sweetness. Brut, the most common grade in Great Britain and the U.S., has 0% to 1.5% shipping dosage. Extra Dry, the next grade, is confusing because it is really sweeter than Brut, with 1% to 2% dosage; then come the sweeter grades, Dry or Sec (2% - 4%) and Demi-Sec (4% - 6%), followed by the rather cloying Doux (8 % - 10%), which is rarely sold in Great Britain and the U.S. Brut non-vintage is the workhorse of all the Champagne houses.

Here are the leading Champagne firms, in descending order of their approximate production and their annual sales worldwide:

Moët & Chandon (White Star, Brut Imperial)
G.H. Mumm (Cordon Rouge)
Piper-Heidsieck
Veuve Clicquot (Yellow Label)
Taittinger (La Francaise)
Perrier-Jouët
Laurent-Perrier
Bollinger
Lanson (Black Label, Ivory Label)
Pommery & Grëno
Charles Heidsieck
Louis Roederer
Pol Roger
Deutz & Geldermann
Nicolas Feuillatte (U.C.V.C.)
Billecart-Salmon
Henriot
A. Charbaut & Fils
Philipponnat
Mercier
Jacquart
Canard-Duchêne
Heidsieck Monopole
Krug (Grande Cuvée)
Ayala
Jacquesson

The pride of certain Champagne houses are the so-called "prestige cuvées," whereby selected lots of wines made in outstanding vintages are given special handling and aging, and are released later than usual. The famous antique bottle used for Dom Pérignon, the flagship of Moët & Chandon, is known all over the world; less widespread, but no less good, is the select Comte de Champagne of the house of Taittinger. Both these prestige cuvées are famous as a Blanc de Blancs; they may also be available in rosé versions. Veuve Clicquot introduced a "Grande Dame" prestige cuvée about ten years ago that has become very popular. It was named for Widow Veuve Clicquot who revolutionized Champagne with the method of remuage (riddling). The exquisite "Fleur de France" prestige cuvée from Perrier-Jouët seduces with its subtlety, not with brute force.

🍃 Alsace 🍃

The vineyards of Alsace lie in a pretty area along the eastern slopes of the Vosges Mountains, near the German border. While Alsace growers do share some German traditions and grape varieties, the area is very much a part of France and most of the wines are fermented dry, in the French style. The city of Strasbourg is the region's capital, but most of the vineyards lie further south, extending in a relatively narrow band along the Vosges, past the cities of Colmar and Mulhouse.

Virtually all Alsace wines are white – a function of the climate and the grape

Above: Rémi Krug, one of two brothers who manage the world famous house of Krug in Champagne.

Left: A bottle of Riesling embellishes this house in the quaint village of Colmar, Alsace.

Above right: The village of Kayserberg in Alsace, one of the most celebrated of all the Alsace wine villages.

varieties grown. Alsace wines differ from most other French regions in that the wines are usually sold with the name of the informing grape variety, instead of a town or vineyard. By law, they must be 100% varietal, and grown only in delimited vineyards. Usually the two best varieties are Riesling, which gives the same fine results here as it does in Germany; and Gewürztraminer, whose full, spicy wines are excellent with Alsace cuisine.

Another superior grape is Pinot Gris (also called Tokay d'Alsace), which gives rounded, scented white wines with considerable character. The fruitiest and grapiest wines usually come from Muscat d'Alsace. The Pinot Blanc of Burgundy, also called Klevner, gives excellent results in Alsace, and may be a good substitute for expensive white Burgundy. Sylvaner is also reliable, but is usually the least of the group. Occasionally the rare Pinot Noir, or Spätburgunder, is grown for light red wines.

Wine laws in Alsace are quite comprehensive. The term Grand Cru, or great growth, relates to 45 individual vineyards who clearly produce superior wine. Additionally, if picked later in the season, better quality wine may qualify as vendange tardive, indicating late harvesting, and the best of these, from individually picked berries, may be sold as sélection des grains nobles. They relate to rare and rather expensive wines that represent the best Alsace has to offer.

Although the vineyards begin near Strasbourg, the best section actually starts southwest of the town of Sélestat, along the "Route du Vin" or wine road that includes all the famous Alsace wine towns. The pretty towns of Ribeauvillé and Riquewihr are especially celebrated, along with Turckheim, Münster and Eguisheim. Certain individual vineyards, such as Trimbach's Clos St. Hune and Schlumberger's Kessler and Kitterlé, are sold under their own name along with the informing grape variety. These can be sensational in great vintages. Further south, the towns of Rouffach, Westhalten and Guebwiller are also notable – the Clos St. Landelin, a single vineyard owned by Muré, makes outstanding wines. The city of Mulhouse marks the southern limit of the Alsace vineyards.

Good Producers:

F. & E. Trimbach, Hugel, Domaine Weinbach, Zind-Humbrecht, Léon Beyer, Schlumberger, Dopff & Irion, Willm, Pierre Sparr, Kunz-Bas, Ostertag, Boeckel, Klipfel, Gustav Lorenz, Muré-Erhard.

❧ The Loire Valley ❧

The Loire is one of France's principal waterways. During the long journey from its source in the Auvergne to its mouth at Nantes, the Loire traverses some especially beautiful countryside and describes some superb sites for vineyards. Long known for its rich scenery and historic castles, the Loire boasts a number of excellent wines.

There are three principal vineyard areas in the Loire. Upstream, in the area known as the upper Loire or Berry, lie the regions of Pouilly-sur-Loire and Sancerre, whose wines have been traditional favorites in Paris restaurants. Further downstream, in a rather broad area surrounding the cities of Orléans and Tours, is the Touraine – a paradise for tourists and wine lovers. Finally, further downstream, is the lower Loire, describing the area around Anjou and Nantes.

The upper Loire chiefly relies on Sauvignon Blanc, known locally as Blanc Fumé, for lively, racy white wines. Sauvignon gives the fresh, grapey character of Pouilly-Fumé and Sancerre, a treat to drink in their youth. Most of the production comes from Sauvignon, but in Sancerre a little Pinot Noir is grown for some elegant reds and fresh rosés. In good vintages they recall light reds from Burgundy, but rarely do they reach the same heights.

Good Producers:

Pouilly-Fumé:
Château de Nozet (de la Doucette)
Château de Tracy
Michel Redde
Didier Dagueneau
Gaudry
Chatelain

Sancerre:
Lucien Crochet
Henri Bourgeois
Paul Cotat
Alphonse Mellot (Domaine La Moussière)
Archambault
Jean-Max Roger
Vincent Delaporte
Château de Sancerre (Marnier-Lapostolle)
Thomas Père et Fils
Roger Neveu
Bailly-Reverdy

Touraine

The area around Tours has been growing wine for centuries. The important difference between this area and Berry is that the white grapes change from Sauvignon to Chenin Blanc, and the reds turn from Pinot Noir to Cabernet Franc, making for dramatic differences in the wines. Touraine is the general appellation for all wine types, and applies to red, white and rosé wines. There are certain sites in this area that grow superior wines, and are entitled to their own appellations: the best sites include Touraine-Amboise, Touraine-Mesland, Touraine-Azay-le-Rideau, and Touraine-Cheverny.

Chenin Blanc, known locally as Pineau de la Loire, has a fresh, flowery

Left: Pasting labels at Domaine Weinbach, Alsace, a process that is still performed here by hand.

Below: In beautiful Riquewihr, one of the most central of the Alsace wine towns, there are many tasting opportunities.

Right: Turckheim, another Alsace wine town, is seen here with the Vosges mountains as a backdrop.

flavor. Its wines are usually best when not entirely dry: this is the case with the popular white wine Vouvray, grown east of Tours, which is capable of maturing for decades in bottle. When conditions are right, some Vouvrays are harvested late in the season and are among the world's greatest dessert wines. Otherwise, because of the high natural acidity of its wines, many Vouvrays are also made sparkling.

Loire Valley reds used to be compared to better Bordeaux, but nowadays most are made to be drunk young. The four best vineyard areas for Cabernet Franc are at Chinon, Bourgueil, St. Nicolas-de-Bourgueil and Saumur-Champigny. The fresh, quaffable red wines grown in these areas are delicious when served chilled.

Good Producers:

Gaston Huet, Vouvray
Château de Moncontour, Vouvray
Prince Philippe Poniatowski, Clos Baudoin
Allias, Vouvray
Marc Brédif, Vouvray
Couly-Dutheil, Chinon
Audebert, Bourgueil
De L'Ile-Boucard, Bourgueil
Charles Joguet, Chinon
Olga Raffault, Chinon
Filliatreau, Saumur-Champigny

In addition to Vouvray, Chenin Blanc finds two especially good vineyard areas further downstream. One is at the Coulée de Serrant, a tiny but beautifully exposed parcel of land owned by the Joly family; adjacent is the area of Savennières, where the natural fruitiness of Chenin Blanc is expressed successfully as a dry wine. Chenin reaches its apogee in a series of small river valleys further downstream, where three select vineyard areas – Quarts de Chaume, Bonnezeaux and Côteaux du Layon – each have their own appellation. Some rare but superb late-harvested Chenin Blanc is grown here, in certain estates where the climate and the exposure are ideal for producing this type of wine.

But the best known wine from this area is Muscadet, made from a grape of the same name. It has become very popular as an inexpensive substitute for white Burgundy. The fine, fresh white wines that it gives have good fruit and acidity, and are produced via the "sur lie" method of leaving the wines in contact with the lees for an extended period after they are made. This practice adds to the wines' freshness and complexity.

The best Muscadets come from the area described by two rivers, the Sevre and Maine, which is the central and best part of the growing area. Most of the basic wine is just sold as "Muscadet," without any indication of area; even so, it can still be very good.

Good Producers:

Joly, Clos de la Coulée de Serrant
Château la Roche aux Moines, Savennières
Château de Belle-Rive, Quarts de Chaume
Château de Suronde, Quarts de Chaume
Sauvion & Fils (Château du Cléray, Muscadet)
Chéreau-Carré, Muscadet'
Barré, Muscadet
Château de la Ragotière, Muscadet
Marcel Sautejeu (Château de L'Hyvinière, Muscadet)
Donatien Bahuaud, Muscadet
Marquis de Goulaine, Muscadet

❧ Rhône ❧

The Rhône is France's international waterway, drawing its source in Switzerland as it courses due south towards the Mediterranean. Over the centuries, wind

Left: A detail of the beautiful Renaissance architecture of the Château de Goulaine, a leading estate in the Muscadet district.

Right: The celebrated Château de Nozay in Pouilly-sur-Loire, owned by the Ladoucette family, is a landmark in the area.

and erosion helped shape some excellent vineyard sites that now grow world-famous wines. A good part of the Rhône region is mountainous, and for this reason the word "côtes," indicating hillsides, is used in the most basic appellation, Côtes-du-Rhône. This term describes red, white and rosé wines grown throughout the Rhône district.

A better grade of Rhône wines is Côtes-du-Rhône Villages, named for certain townships in the Rhône district that have been shown to grow wines of superior quality. The name of the township, or village, appears after the Côtes-du-Rhône appellation (e.g. Côtes-du-Rhône Chusclan). These are among the best values in French wines today – they are sturdy, reliable and usually not too expensive.

Many centuries of experience among Rhône winegrowers has shown that not all grape varieties ripen at the same rate, and conditions in some vintages favor certain varieties over others. Vintners have also found that a mix of different varieties gives a better balanced wine: some grapes may have color but not enough acid, while others may have plenty of alcohol but are lacking in fruit and aroma. For this reason, in most vineyards several different varieties are planted. From about 75,000 acres of vineyard, about two-thirds of the production is in red wine.

For red wines, there are four principal varieties. Syrah, said to be named for the city of Shiraz in Persia, its original home, is used for all the great red Rhône wines, either on its own or in blends with other varieties. It has a deep crimson color, considerable body, and a characteristic spiciness. Grenache, which is grown throughout the Mediterranean, is a sweet grape without much color; hence it is well-suited for making rosés, or supple red wines to which Syrah or other varieties will be added. Mourvèdre, a popular Rhône variety, is a deep-colored variety that adds character in blends. Cinsault, a grape with plenty of color but usually not much tannin or acidity, puts the finishing touches on the blends of different varieties for the Rhône red wines.

Long a distant second to the red wines and the rosés, Rhône whites have made a comeback recently. Unfortunately, the best white Rhône variety, Viognier, is very rare and expensive. It is only grown in certain sections of the northern Rhône, to make the exquisite white wines of Château-Grillet and Condrieu. Another white varietal nearly as popular is Marsanne, which is responsible for the celebrated whites of Hermitage and Crozes-Hermitage; in adjacent vineyards a supplementary variety, Roussanne, may also be grown.

The Rhône vineyards have been very

Left: The hilltop village of Sancerre, as seen from the nearby township of Chavignol in the Loire.

Below left: Clos de L'Echo, one of the top holdings of Domaine Couly-Dutheil in Chinon. Here is a stand of new Cabernet Franc vines.

Below: Village and château of Chinon, as seen from the River Vienne.

precisely delimited over the centuries. Only the best, southern exposed slopes are set aside for the top vineyards, many of which are quite small; although the area as a whole is quite productive. For simplicity, we can group the Rhône into two principal vineyard areas: northern, around the towns of Ampuis and Vienne, and southern, about 120 km to the south, spreading out over a wide area north of Marseilles.

The little vineyard area of Côte Rotie, referred to as "the roasted slope" because of its excellent exposure to the sun, lies adjacent to the town of Ampuis and produces full, exquisite red wines, almost exclusively from Syrah. Hermitage, known a century ago as the "manliest" of French wines, is similar. It is produced on a single, ideally exposed hillside just outside Tain-L'Hermitage. It is surrounded by a much larger area known as Crozes-Hermitage, which grows similar but less exalted red and white wines, in which Syrah and Marsanne play the predominant roles in the blends.

One of the most famous of all French vineyard estates is the tiny parcel known as Château-Grillet. Here, on terraced hillsides, is one of the smallest appellation contrôlées in France – and one of its most exquisite white wines. Nearby, in a larger growing area, the vineyards of Condrieu, shared by many different growers, produce similarly fine and expensive wines. Other areas in the northern Rhône are also important. Cornas, a slender ribbon of vineyard high above the Rhône, makes intense, concentrated red wines exclusively from Syrah; Saint Joseph, further downstream, produces lighter but similar wines, from a wider area.

THE WORLD OF WINE

Left: An old vineyard in Muscadet near the township of Le Landreau, in the heart of the Sèvre-et-Maine area.

Right: Harvesting Syrah grapes in the northern Côtes-du-Rhône, in the Crozes-Hermitage area

Good Producers:

Marcel Guigal
Jean-Louis Chave
Paul Jaboulet (La Chapelle)
Auguste Clape
Marc Chapoutier (Mure de la Suzerane, Chante Alouette)
Delas Frères
Georges Vernay
J. Gerin
Vidal-Fleury
Dervieux-Thaize

Most of the wine sold as Côtes-du-Rhône comes from a wide area to the south, where Syrah gives way to more supple, productive varieties. They may be sold by the individual producer, under the name of the estate, as "négociant" wines, sold under the name of the shipper, or as branded wines. In general, the best Côtes-du-Rhônes come from individual vineyards which will state "mis en bouteilles à la propriété" on the label.

Two new appellations are now appearing on world markets. One is Côteaux du Tricastin, near the area of Montélimar; another is Côtes du Ventoux, in the southernmost section, along the southern flanks of the Mont du Ventoux. Red wines from either appellation can often be more interesting than ordinary Côtes-du-Rhône, and better value than some of the best known appellations.

The most famous southern Rhône wine is Châteauneuf-du-Pape, named for the "new château of the pope" when the church relocated its seat to France during medieval times. Much of the soil in Châteauneuf-du-Pape is composed of large, rounded pebbles, which hold the sun's heat after hours and offer excellent drainage. As many as thirteen grape varieties are authorized for Châteauneuf-du-Pape. In recent years a little white Châteauneuf-du-Pape has been offered.

There is no set formula for grapes in Châteauneuf-du-Pape. Some properties have a high proportion of Grenache, which makes for a lighter, more alcoholic wine; others rely more on Mourvèdre and Cinsault. Syrah is important here, but so are the white varieties. Growers in Châteauneuf-du-Pape tend to have very high quality standards, and ship their wines in a special embossed bottle with a seal on the glass. A neighboring wine district, Gigondas, has recently emerged as a major challenger to Châteauneuf and the wines are usually much less expensive.

Rosé wines are popular in the Rhône because they complement the superb seafood of the Mediterranean. Adjacent to Châteauneuf-du-Pape is Tavel, where the growers have long specialized in rosé production. Sweet white wines are another specialty of the Rhône. In the area of Beaumes-de-Venise, a little Muscat is grown for a sensational sweet wine known as Muscat de Beaumes-de-Venise.

Good Producers:

Château de Beaucastel (Perrin)
Château Rayas
Vieux Télégraphe
Château Fortia
Marcel Guigal
Clos l'Oratoire des Papes
Château Maucoux
Domaine de Mont-Redon
Château des Fines-Roches
Chante-Perdrix
Château de la Nerthe
Paul Jaboulet
Nativelle (Domaine de Coyeaux)

Left: View from the Côte Rôtie "roasted slope" near Ampuis. This steep little slope produces some of the finest reds of the northern Rhône.

Right: Another view from the Côte Rôtie, showing how the vines are trained on stakes.

❧ Provence ❧

In addition to being one of the most scenic areas in France (its Mediterranean vistas are unsurpassed), Provence has some excellent wine districts. Historically, Châteauneuf-du-Pape is considered a part of Provence, but nowadays it is more proper to refer to it as a Rhône wine. As the vineyards spread out southeast, towards the cities of Aix and Nice, some delicious wines are grown – many of them still not too expensive.

The most basic place-name, Côtes de Provence, which describes red, white and rosé wines, became an appellation contrôlée in 1978 – many years after other French wine districts. Prior to this time, wines sold under this name often cost next to nothing, and many were delicious. But with the enactment of AOC, most of the growers began asking more for their wines, "since they were now worth more than before." This curious rationale was fortunately accompanied by an overall improvement in quality, and while Côtes de Provence wines may no longer be cheap, they have never been better.

Most of the wines are reds and rosés, made from Mourvèdre, Cinsault, and a little Carignan. The light, fresh rosés are a delight – often among the best in all of France. They are refreshing, bone-dry and have a fruitiness that is a perfect match to the superb seafood dishes of Provence.

The best Provence wine districts have had their own appellations for many years. Bandol, one of the most famous, describes red, white and rosé wines from a village of the same name; the reds and rosés are the best, particularly from Domaine Tempier. Cassis (which has nothing to do with the liqueur) is another; its fresh, faintly resiny white wines are ideal accompaniments to Provencal cuisine. Bellet, a district surrounding the city of Nice, may be enjoyed when visiting the city, but since the Nicois enjoy the wine even more than the tourists, not much remains for export.

❧ Languedoc/Roussillon ❧

Languedoc, also known as the "Pays d'Oc," is a very old province in southwestern France that has been attracting a great deal of attention in recent years. Long a producer of ordinary wines that were rarely sold with any indication of appellation, the region has been extensively replanted in better grape varieties and is now an important source of reasonably priced wine for export.

The traditional name of this important region is the Midi, extending in a broad area west of the city of Marseilles in a giant sweep, reaching the seacoast city of Perpignan near the Spanish border. It describes the important departments of Gard, Hérault, Aude and Pyrénées-Orientales, which jointly include over 400,000 acres of vineyard.

Grapes traditional to the area are similar to those of the Côtes-du-Rhône, except that standards are somewhat less rigid here. White wines may be produced from such venerable varieties as Clairette and Ugni Blanc, which produce soft wines that mature rapidly. Reds may be grown from Cinsault, Mourvèdre or Grenache, depending on the soil and the

vineyard in question. In the past, the mainstay of the area's red wine production had traditionally been Carignan, which is productive but gives a fairly straightforward wine.

But a revolution has come to the area. These varieties have been steadily displaced by better grapes such as Chardonnay and Viognier for white wines, and Cabernet Sauvignon and Merlot for reds – the sort of wines that today's consumers are looking for.

There are many appellations in this venerable area. Some were elevated from former V.D.Q.S. status in the 1970s, but others still remain in the lower category, waiting their turn. Here are a few of the townships with good wines:

Clairette de Bellegard
Costières de Gard
Faugères
Saint-Chinian

Left: The unique soil at Châteauneuf-du-Pape is composed of rocks that drain easily and retain the sun's heat after dark which helps the grapes to ripen.

Right: The peaks of the Montmirail, towering over some old vines in the Gigondas area, define some especially good vineyards.

Below: Ripe Syrah grapes, ready for harvest in Châteauneuf-du-Pape.

Left: The village of Sablet, one of the celebrated wine towns in the Côtes-du-Rhône area.

Right: Wine tasting in Cairanne, Provence.

Below: Fitou vintner Jean Valzi in the Languedoc/Roussillon area, showing off some recent vintages.

Côteaux du Languedoc
Minervois
Corbières
Fitou
Côtes du Roussillon
Côtes du Roussillon-Villages.

In addition, the Midi as a whole has an old reputation for sweet fortified wines, particularly Muscats; Muscat de Frontignan and Muscat de Lunel are well-known examples of this type, while Banyuls, grown near the city of Perpignan, more closely resembles Ports.

Good Producers:

Fortant de France, Vignerons Catalans, Beyssière, Château Gourgazaud, Georges Bonfils, Château Ricardelle, and numerous caves coopératives.

GERMANY

Grown in a cool climate with a short growing season, German wines are unmatched for their delicacy and scent. They rarely exceed 9% alcohol, and while they have been traditionally finished with a bit of sweetness, many German wine producers are now making wines that tend to be somewhat drier than they used to be.

All German wines are regulated by the 1971 German Wine Law, which stipulates how they may be sold. The German Wine Law recognizes thirteen growing areas, known as Anbaugebiete (regions under cultivation), which jointly make up about 250,000 acres of vineyards. Listed alphabetically, they are: Ahr (wines that are rarely seen outside the district), Baden, Franken, Hessische Bergstrasse (wines that are rarely seen outside the district), Mittelrhein, Mosel-Saar-Ruwer, Nahe, Rheingau, Rheinhessen, Rheinpfalz, Sachsen and Saale-Unstrut (too soon to judge these last two wine districts, which were added after the unification of West and East Germany in 1990) and Württemberg.

Within each Anbaugebiet lies at least one sub-region, known as a Bereich, which can contain many hundred acres of vineyard. The name of each Bereich relates to popular wines in the trade, and certain basic wines can be sold under the name of the Bereich (e.g., Bereich Nierstein, Bereich Bernkastel). Since these wines are extensively blended, they do not represent the ultimate in German wines but are usually good values. Each Bereich can be made up of one or more collective vineyard sites, known as Grosslagen, which relate to traditional wine names in order to allow some blending by the producers. Because a wine sold under a Grosslage sounds like an individual vineyard site but actually is a group of several different vineyards, many producers feel it is deceptive. However, since some blending between vineyards is allowed, many of the Grosslagen wines are moderately priced. An individual vineyard site is known as an Einzellage under the wine law, and its legal minimum size is 5 hectares (12 acres).

White wines make up about 85% of German wine production, although recently there has been a renewed interest in German reds and rosés. Traditionally, the most famous German wines have been grown from Riesling, which gives its

Far left: A basket of Silvaner grapes, picked from a vineyard in the southern Rhine district.

Left: The church spire in the village of Graach on the Mosel. Many top vineyards can be seen in the background.

best in a cool climate with a late growing season. But Riesling may be supplanted by another native German variety, Silvaner (Sylvaner), especially in warmer districts; recently there has been renewed interest in Pinot Blanc, known as Weissburgunder, which gives excellent wines that are like many Chardonnays from France and California.

About a century ago, German scientists developed a whole series of new grapes. The first of these was Müller-Thurgau, named for the grape specialist who developed it, and by 1996 fully one-fourth of all acreage in Germany was devoted to Müller-Thurgau. The grape is productive, and is mostly used for popularly priced blends from the Rhine regions. Another well-known example is the Scheurebe, whose wines typically have a full, grapey flavor.

German red wines have long been regarded as a curiosity. While most tend to be rather light, the best reds come from Spätburgunder (Pinot Noir): good examples are grown in the Rheingau, particularly Assmannshausen, and in Hessia (Ingelheim), the Ahr, and the Pfalz (Bad Dürkheim). An even greater variety of rosés originate from the same variety. Another red grape, Portuguieser, plays an important role in the Pfalz.

German wines are graded by their degree of ripeness. In most of the world's wine districts, grapes reach the necessary sugar content on their own; in Germany, the grapes usually have to have sugar added in order to reach the proper alcohol. This is the same process of sugaring, or chaptalization, that is sanctioned for use in France and Austria, but not in Italy, Spain or California.

The most basic grade of German wine is called Tafelwein, or table wine, which is a blend of wines to which sugar is nor-

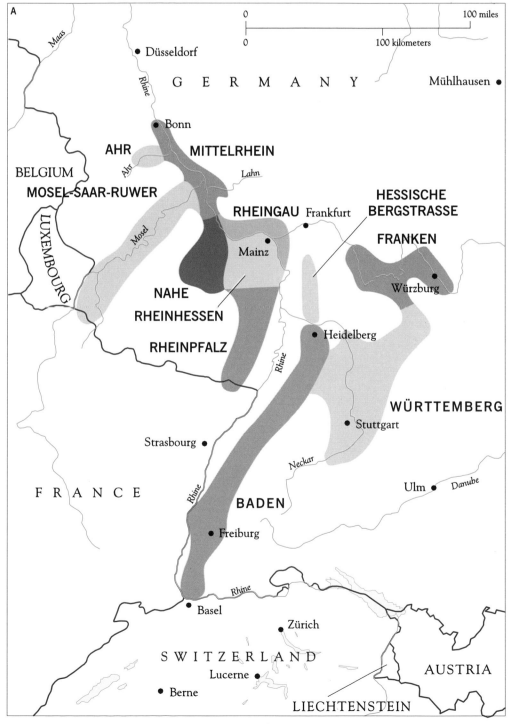

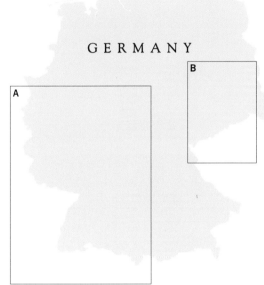

mally added. A Tafelwein carries no other geographic designation. A step above it is Landwein, which is a higher quality table wine from designated wine-producing districts but it is still a basic quality grade.

A more important category is Qualitätswein, or quality wine, whose full name is Qualitätswein bestimmter Anbaugebiete or QbA for short. By law, these come from one of the designated Anbaugebiete, and must meet minimum quality standards. The grapes must achieve a minimum sugar content before picking, but some sugaring is allowed to reach the necessary levels of ripeness. For this reason, wines sold as QbAs are usually inexpensive and represent a grower's basic offerings. A new quality grade used by some growers on the Mosel is Hochgewächs, or noble growth, relating to select lots of QbAs that are of clearly superior quality.

The best German wines are sold under the designation "Qualitätswein mit Prädikat," or quality wine with distinction. Prädikat wines must originate from fully ripened grapes and may not be produced with any sugar added. There are six levels of Prädikat wines, in ascending order of quality:

Kabinett, drier and less expensive offerings; suitable for meals.

Spätlese, late-harvested wines, richer and a bit sweeter.

Auslese, select late harvest wines, made from a selection of ripe bunches in which unripe grapes have been removed. Quite sweet.

Beerenauslese, or berry selection, made from a selection of individual ripe grapes. Very sweet and quite expensive.

Left: Nikolaus Wegeler-Deinhard, of the famous Deinhard family that produces top wines in the Mosel and Rhine districts.

Right: The Deidesheimer Hof, in the village of Deidesheim/Rheinpfalz, is one of the top restaurants in the region. Their wine list is as celebrated as their menu.

THE GERMAN WINE LABEL

The specified growing region: one of the 13 designated regions in Germany.

The quality level of the wine, indicating ripeness of the grapes at harvest.

Wines bottled and produced by the grower or a cooperative of growers may be labelled "Erzeugerabfüllung". Estates and growers can use "Gutsabfüllung" as an alternative. Other wineries and bottlers are indentified as "Abfüller."

The official testing number: proof that the wine has passed chemical and sensory testing required for all German Quality Wines.

The town and the vineyard from which the grapes come.

The grape variety.

The year in which the grapes were harvested.

The taste or style of the wine. In this case, sweet. If it were trocken, it would be dry. If there is no indication the wine usually offers a harmonious balance of sweetness and acidity.

MOSEL · SAAR · RUWER

Der Weinbergsbesitz von
Dr. Pauly
umfaßt Lagen in Bernkastel, Graach, Wehlen, Zeltingen, Erden und Brauneberg.

Qualitätswein mit Prädikat

Erzeuger-Abfüllung

A. P. Nr.
2 576 185 040 86

375 ml

1985
Bernkasteler Badstube Riesling Eiswein
Weingut Dr. Pauly-Bergweiler
Zach. Bergweiler-Prüm Erben · Bernkastel

❧ Mosel-Saar-Ruwer ❧

The Mosel district is made up of three different and distinct areas, and the Anbaugebiet is known officially as Mosel-Saar-Ruwer. Mosel wines are especially prized for their scent and their delicacy. The lightest generally come from the Saar Valley; Ruwer wines are similarly delicate and very refined in style. The Mittel-Mosel is the largest section of the three, with most of the famous wine towns hugging the banks of the Mosel river.

The best wines originate in the following towns and vineyards, identified with leading growers (in each instance, the Grosslage name for a group of towns will be identified, to distinguish it from an individual site):

Saar

Scharzhofberger (technically an Ortsteil, or part of a community; always sold under its own name)
Wiltingen (Kupp, Braunfels, Braune Kupp, Klosterberg, Hölle, Gottesfuss, Rosenberg, Schlossberg, Sandberg)
Ockfen (Bockstein, Herrenberg)
Wawern (Herrenberg)
Kanzem (Altenberg, Hörecker, Schlossberg, Sonnenberg)
Oberemmel (Hütte, Altenberg, Agritiusberg, Karlsberg, Rosenberg)
Ayl (Kupp, Scheidterberg, Herrenberger)
Serrig (Vogelsang, Heiligenborn, Saarfelser Schlossberg, Antoniusberg, Heiligenborn, Hoeppslei)
GROSSLAGE (for entire Saar district): Wiltinger Scharzberg

Good Producers:

Egon Müller, Scharzhof
Le Gallais, Kanzem
Vereinigte Hospitien, Trier
Bischöflichen Weingüter, Trier (three separate domaines, each one excellent)
Verewaltung der Staatlichen Weinbaudomäne, Trier
Reichsgraf von Kesselstatt
von Hövel, Oberemmel
Dr. Fischer, Ockfen
Adolf Rheinart, Ockfen
Gebrüder Kramp, Ayl

Trockenbeerenauslese, or dried berry selection, made from individual ripe grapes that have become highly concentrated. Intensely sweet, rare and extremely expensive.
Eiswein, or ice wine, made from frozen grapes harvested late in the season. In the process, the water freezes but not the sugar or the acid: the grapes are gently crushed and the resulting sweet wine is a rich, exotic nectar. Very expensive. By law, must reach minimum standards for Beerenauslese.

In the more basic quality grades, drier styles of German wines have been developed that are more appropriate with food. Normally, German wines are finished with a bit of sweetness to a balance out their acidity. Such a wine is known as a "lieblich" or "mild" wine. By withholding the sweetness and allowing the wine to ferment out to dryness, a drier version can be made. German wines that are essentially dry are sold as "trocken" (dry); if they have slightly more sweetness, they may be labelled "halbtrocken" (semi-dry). The exact designation is determined officially by the ratio of sugar to acidity, and applies to all of the grades of Qualitätswein.

The origins of German wines can be easily determined by the color of the bottle: green for Mosels, brown for Rhines. In addition, there is the squat Bocksbeutel bottle used for the wines of Franken and the Badisches Frankenland district of Baden, which is always green.

Ruwer

Maximin Grünhaus (von Schubert, sole proprietor)
Eitelsbacher Karthäuserhofberg (Tyrell, sole proprietor)
Eitelsbach (Marienholz)
Kasel (Nieschen, Kehrnagel, Herrenberg, Hitzlay, Paulinsberg, Timpert)
Avelsbach (Hammerstein, Altenberg, Herrenberg)
Waldrach (Krone, Hubertusberg, Meisenberg, Ehrenberg, Jesuitengarten)
GROSSLAGE: Trierer Römerlay

Good Producers:

von Schubert (Maximin Grünhaus)
Tyrell, Eitelsbach
Karlsmühle, Mertesdorf
Reichsgraf von Kesselstatt

Mittel-Mosel

Zell
GROSSLAGE: Zeller Schwarze Katz
Ürzig (Würzgarten)
Erden (Treppchen, Prälat)
GROSSLAGE: Ürziger Schwarzlay
Zeltingen (Sonnenuhr, Schlossberg)
Wehlen (Sonnenuhr, Nonnenberg, Klosterberg)
Graach (Himmelreich, Domprobst, Abtsberg, Josephshöfer)
GROSSLAGE: Wehlener Münzlay
Bernkastel (Doktor, Lay, Bratenhöfchen, am Doktorberg, Johannisbrünnen, Schlossberg)
GROSSLAGE: Bernkasteler Badstube
Brauneberg (Juffer, Juffer-Sonnenuhr)
Kues (Kardinalsberg)
Kesten (Paulinhofsberg)
GROSSLAGE: Bernkasteler Kurfürstlay
Longuich

GROSSLAGE: Longuicher Probtsberg
Piesport (Goldtröpfchen, Lay)
GROSSLAGE: Piesporter Michelsberg
Trittenheim (Apotheke, Altärchen)

Good Producers:

Dr. Thanisch (Knabben-Spier)
J.J. Prüm
Dr. Loosen, Bernkastel
Reichsgraf von Kesselstatt
Friedrich-Wilhelm Gymnasium
Bischöflichen Weingüter, Trier
S.A. Prüm
Studert-Prüm
Lauerburg, Bernkastel
Wegeler-Deinhard
Heribert Kerpen, Wehlen
Willi Schaefer, Graach
Dr. Pauly-Bergweiler (Peter Nicolay)
Selbach-Oster (shippers wines: J. & H. Selbach label)
Merkelbach
Christoffel Erben
Fritz Haag, Brauneberg
Weller-Lehnert, Piesport
Reuscher-Haardt, Piesport
Zentralkellerei der MittelMosel (Moselland)

Rhine

In contrast, the Rhine region is much larger and more spread out. Much of the ordinary blending wine comes from the Rheinhessen and Rheinpfalz, in the form of Liebfraumilch or Niersteiner Gutes Domtal, but there are scores of select estates that produce excellent wines at reasonable prices.

❧ Rheingau ❧

The Rheingau is unique among the German growing districts. It is protected to the south by the Rhine itself, which helps regulate the climate; to the north it is shielded by the Taunus Mountains. Consequently, the area has long been noted for its high-quality wine, to the point where Rheingau and Riesling are synonymous with each other. Here is a roster of the Rheingau's leading vineyards:

Assmannshausen (mostly light, expensive red wines)
Rüdesheim (best vineyards are located

Right: Overview of the town of Bernkastel from the famous Doctor vineyard. This photo clearly illustrates the extremely steep slopes that are a major factor in the high quality of the wine.

on the Rüdesheimer Berg, and are so designated):

Berg Rottland
Berg Roseneck
Berg Schlossberg

then come a bevy of other good vineyards in Rüdesheim:

Bischofsberg
Drachenstein
Kirchenpfad
Magdalenenkreuz
Klosterlay
Klosterberg
GROSSLAGE: Rüdesheimer Burgweg
Geisenheim (Mäuerchen, Rothenberg, Kläuserweg, Mönchspfad, Kilzberg, Fuchsberg, Schlossgarten)
Schloss Johannisberg (Ortsteil, sold under its own name)

Johannisberg (Klaus, Vogelsang, Hölle, Mittelhölle, Hansenberg, Goldatzel, Schwarzenstein)
Winkel (Hasensprung, Jesuitengarten, Gutenberg, Dachsberg, Bienengarten, Schlossberg, Honigberg)
GROSSLAGE: Johannisberger Erntebringer
Schloss Vollrads (Ortsteil, sold under its own name)
Hallgarten (Jungfer, Schönhell, Hendelberg, Wurzgarten)
GROSSLAGE: Hallgartener Mehrhölzchen
Mittelheim (Edelmann, St. Nikolaus)
Oestrich (Lenchen, Doosberg, Klosterberg)
Steinberg (Ortsteil, sold under its own name)

Hattenheim (Mannberg, Pfaffenberg, Wisselbrunnen, Engelmannsberg)
Erbach (Marcobrunn, Siegelsberg, Schlossberg, Hohenrain, Steinmorgen, and Michelmark)
Kiedrich (Sandgrub, Gräfenberg)
Eltville (Sonnenberg, Langenstuck, Taubenberg, Rheinberg, and Sandgrub)
Rauenthal (Baiken, Gehrn, Wülfen, Rothenberg, Langenstück and Nonnenberg)
Walluf (Berg Bildstock, Langenstück, Walkenberg, Oberberg and Fitusberg)
GROSSLAGE: Rauenthaler Steinmächer
Hochheim (Domdechaney, Kirchenstück, Hölle, Hofmeister, Stielweg, Stein, Königin Viktoriaberg)
GROSSLAGE: Hochheimer Daubhaus

Below left: Tractors can be used for many different functions in Germany: tilling, leaf trimming, even machine harvesting. This one belongs to Deinhard in the Pfalz.

Good Producers:

Schloss Groenesteyn, Rüdesheim
Georg Breuer, Rüdesheim
Schloss Johannisberg (Metternich)
Johannishof (Eser)
G.H. von Mumm, Johannisberg
Landgraf von Hessen, Winkel
Schloss Vollrads, Winkel
Schloss Schönborn, Hattenheim
Schloss Reinhartshausen, Erbach
Robert Weil, Kiedrich
Langwerth von Simmern, Eltville
Freiherr zu Knyphausen, Eltville
Staatsweingüter, Eltville
Weingut Balthasar Ress, Eltville
Domdechant Werner, Hochheim
Weingut Hupfeld Erben (Königin Viktoriaberg)

❀ Rheinhessen ❀

Rheinhessen, or Hessia, is the largest of the German wine districts, and climatically the most diverse. The best vineyards are generally close to the Rhine, along a narrow band known as the Rhine Front. They include the following townships:

Bingen (Scharlachberg, Kirchberg, Schlossberg-Swätzerchen)
GROSSLAGE: Binger St. Rochuskapelle
Nackenheim (Rothenberg, Engelsberg, Schmitts-Kapelle)
Nierstein (Pettenthal, Brudersberg, Kranzberg, Orbel, Hipping, Ölberg, Glöck, Heiligenbaum, Patersberg, Bildstock)
GROSSLAGE: Niersteiner Auflangen,

Niersteiner Spiegelberg, Niersteiner Rehbach
Oppenheim (Sackträger, Herrenberg, Kreuz, Daubhaus, Schlossberg, Schloss, Gutleuthaus, Paterhof, Herrengarten)
GROSSLAGE: Oppenheimer Kröttenbrunnen
Dienheim (Falkenberg, Herrenberg, Kreuz, Paterhof, Tafelstein)
GROSSLAGE: Niersteiner Gutes Domtal

Good Producers:

von Oehler, Bingen
Gunderloch, Nackenheim
Heyl zu Herrnsheim, Nierstein (sole proprietor: Brudersberg)
Franz-Karl Schmitt, Nierstein
Weingut Strub, Nierstein
Heinrich Braun, Nierstein
Anton Balbach, Nierstein
Georg Albrecht Schneider, Nierstein
Louis Guntrum, Nierstein
Gustav-Adolf Schmitt, Nierstein

Further inland, the soil quickly changes its character and the vineyards get more productive. Formerly, growers in this part of the Rheinhessen just sold their wines to shippers for blending, and the southern Rheinhessen is the original producing area for the popular Liebfraumilch. Broadly, this name applies to a blended, semi-dry wine from the entire Rhine district; specifically, there is a single, select vineyard outside the city of Worms known as the Liebfrauenstifts-Kirchenstück, from which the wine originally derived its name. Many Rhein-

hessen vintners produce excellent wine under their own label and have a ready clientele of wine drinkers. You can expect good, reliable wines from the following areas:

Ingelheim (also good for reds and rosés)
Bornheim (GROSSLAGE Adelberg)
Mainz (GROSSLAGE St. Alban)
Alsheim (GROSSLAGE Rheinblick)
Bechtheim GROSSLAGE Pilgerpfad, Gotteshilfe)
Gau-Bickelheim
Worms: Liebfrauenstifts-Kirchenstück
Bereich Wonnegau

Good Producers:

P.J. Valckenberg, Worms
Langenbach, Worms
H. Sichel Sons, Alzey (the shippers of Blue Nun)
St. Ursula Weinkellerei, Bingen (excellent shippers of regional wines)

❀ Rheinpfalz ❀

The Pfalz, or Palatinate, enjoys a warm, sunny climate that sets it apart from the other areas, and it rarely has bad vintages. While Riesling only figures in a relatively small part of the wine production, there are a number of famous wine towns in the Pfalz, which is divided into two Bereiche: Mittel-Haardt and Südliche Weinstrasse. The Mittel-Haardt has the greatest reputation for Riesling, but the second district has several new growers who have established a strong local following in recent years.

Mittel-Haardt

Kallstadt
GROSSLAGE: Kallstadter Kobnert
Ungstein
GROSSLAGE: Ungsteiner Honigsäckel
Bad Dürkheim (Nonnengaraten, Fuchsmantel, Fronhof, Abtsfronhof)
GROSSLAGE: Dürkheimer Feuerberg
Wachenheim (Gerümpel, Luginsland, Goldbächel, Rechbächel, Bischofsgarten)
Forst (Jesuitengarten, Kirchenstück, Freundstück, Ungeheuer, Pechstein)
GROSSLAGE: Forster Mariengarten
Deidesheim (Hohenmorgen, Kalkofen, Leinhöhle, Herrgottsacker, Kieselberg)

Right: An aerial view of the Liebfrauenkirche church in Worms, which inspired the name Liebfraumilch.

Ruppertsberg (Reiterpfad, Linsenbusch, Gaisböhl, Nussbien, Hoheburg)

Good Producers:

Rainer Lingenfelder, Grosskarlbach
Kohler Ruprecht, Kallstadt
Dr. Karl Schaefer Bad Dürkheim
Fitz-Ritter, Bad Dürkheim
Stumpf-Fitz'sches Wein
gut Annaberg, Bad Dürkheim
Kurt Darting, Bad Dürkheim
Dr. Bürklin-Wolf, Wachenheim
Heinrich Spindler, Forst
Weingut Eugen Müller, Forst
Reichsrat von Buhl, Deidesheim
Weingut Dr. Bassermann-Jordan, Deidesheim
Dr. Deinhard, Deidesheim

Südliche Weinstrasse

Haardt (Mandelgarten, Burgergarten, Herrenletten, Herzog, Mandelring)
Mussbach (Eselshaut)
Siebeldingen

GROSSLAGE: Siebeldinger Königsgarten
Gimmeldingen (Mandelgarten, Schlossel)
GROSSLAGE: Gimmeldinger Meerspinne
Maikammer
Edenkoben
GROSSLAGE: Schloss Ludwigshöhe
Rhodt

Good Producers:

Weingut Müller-Catoir
Weingut Okonomierat Rebholz, Siebeldingen

❧ Nahe ❧

Stylistically, Nahe wines show a synthesis between the lighter Mosels and the heartier Rheingaus; but in fact there are two separate sections of the Nahe that run the entire gamut of German wine types. In the Nahe's lower reaches, near the city of Kreuznach and in the Bereich of the same name, the area borders the

Rheinhessen and many of the wines share similarities. Upstream, the area is cooler and the soil is markedly different, but the protective influence of the river is still there. Here are the leading areas:

Münster-Sarmsheim (Dautenpflänzer, Pittersberg)
Wallhausen
Burg Layen
Dorsheim
GROSSLAGE: Münsterer
Schlosskapelle
Laubenheim (Karthäuser, Krone, St. Remigiusberg)
Langenlonsheim (Königsschild, Lohrer Berg, Steinchen)
Kreuznach (Narrenkappe, Mönchberg, Brückes, Hinkelstein, Krötenpfuhl, Kahlenberg, Steinberg, St. Martin, Kauzenberg, Galgenberg, Tilgesbrunnen)
Roxheim (Höllenberg, Mühlenberg, Berg, Hüttenberg, Sonnenberg)
GROSSLAGE: Kreuznacher Kronenberg
Traisen (Bastei)
Bad Münster (Rotenfelser im Winkel, Höll, Steigerdell, Götzenfels, Königsgarten)
Norheimer (Kafels, Delchen, Klosterfels, Götzenfels, Kirschenheck)
Niederhausen (Hermannshöhle, Rosenberg, Hermannsberg, Steinwingert, Klamm, Rosenheck, Kertz, Pfingstweide)
Schloss Böckelheim (Konigsfels, Kupfergrube, Felsenberg, Heimberg, In den Felsen, Muhlberg)

Good Producers:

August Anheuser, Bad Kreuznach
Paul Anheuser, Bad Kreuznach
Weingut Dr. Höfer, Burg Layen
Schlossgut Diehl, Burg Layen
Weingut Erbhof Tesch, Langenlonsheim
Weingut am Katharinenstift (Familie Korrell)
Kruger-Rumpf, Münster-Sarmsheim
Prinz Salm-Dalberg, Wallhausen
Hans Crusius, Traisen
Staatlichen Weinbaudömane
Niederhausen-Schlossböckelheim
Hermann Dönnhof, Oberhausen
Reichsgraf von Plettenberg
Gutleuthof (Schlink)
Jacob Schneider, Niederhausen

❧ Mittelrhein ❧

The Mittelrhein produces only 1% of German wine but it is one of the most scenic of the wine districts. Its main towns are Bacharach, Boppard and Oberwesel.

Good Producers:

Toni Jost, Adolf Weingart, Ratzenberger.

❧ Franken ❧

Franken (Franconia) is the original home of the squat Bocksbeutel bottle. The vineyards follow the valley of the Main River; the center is the city of Würzburg. The most famous vineyard, Stein, gave its way to Franconian wines in general –they are often referred to as Steinweine. Here is a vineyard roster:
Würzburg (Stein, Leiste, Abtsleite, Innere Leiste, Kirchberg, Stein/Harfe, Pfaffenberg, Schlossberg)
Escherndorf (Lump, Berg, Furstenberg)
Iphofen (Julius Echter-Berg, Kronsberg, Kalb)
Randersacker (Marsberg, Pfulben, Teufelskeller, Sonnenstuhl, Dabug)
Castell (Bausch, Kugelspiel, Kirchberg, Schlossberg, Hohenart, Trautberg)

Above right: An overlook at the broad, fertile plain of the Rheinhessen, whose mild, attractive wines are ideally suited to blending.

Below right: Heinz Bauer, estate manager and winemaker, at his cellars in Deidesheim.

Good Producers:

Burgerspital zum Heiligen Geist,
Würzburg
Furstlich Castell'sches Domänenamt,
Castel
Juliusspital, Würzburg
Weingut Schmitt, Randersacker
Staatliche Hofkellerei, Würzburg

❧ Baden ❧

Baden is the most southerly of the German wine districts, and the region has a
high potential for wine-growing. Until
recently most of the region's production
was controlled by a single wine cooperative, the Zentralkellerei der Badischer
Winzergenossenschaft (mercifully abbre-

viated as Z.B.W.), located in Breisach.
But there are a number of other excellent
estates in the Baden district, which is
very spread out over a large area.

The Baden Bereiche include: Badisches Frankenland, Bergstrasse Kraich-
gau, Ortenau, Breisgau, Kaiserstuhl-
Tuniberg, Markgräflerland, and Bodensee
(Lake Constance).

Good Producers:

Zentralkellerei der Badischer
Winzergenossenschaft (Z.B.W.), Breisach
Versuchs- und Lehrgut Blankenhornsberg,
Ihringen
Weingut Männle, Durbach
Wolff Metternich Weingut, Durbach
Freiherr von Neveu, Durbach
Schloss Staufenberg

❧ Württemberg ❧

Württemberg, traditionally a state associated with Baden to the south, has many
good vineyards but the wines are little
known outside the region.

Good Producers:

Graf Adelmann (Brüssele Spitze),
Kleinbottwar, Graf von Neipperg,
Schwaigern, Fürst zu Hohenlohe-
Ohringen, Ohringen, Weingut von
Gemmingen-Hornberg, Neckarzimmern,
Staatlichen Weinbaudömane, Weinsberg.

ITALY

Italy is the world's greatest vineyard – and the world's greatest producer of wine. Practically every one of the Italian provinces grows wine, from the snow-capped Alps in the north all the way to the arid slopes of Sicily. From a winning combination of superb vineyards and a wine-growing heritage that dates back to Roman times, Italian wines have truly taken the world by storm.

Although Italian wines have been praised for centuries, they have made particular progress during the past three decades. Initially this related to Italy's membership in the European Economic Community (EEC), and as a condition to Italy's joining the union, laws were drafted in order to standardize wine production among the leading member nations. In 1963 Italy drafted the laws of denominazione di origine controllata (D.O.C), which established official boundaries for wine-growing zones, laid out rules for authorized grape varieties in those regions, and set limits on production. Currently over 800 wines have been classified as D.O.C., in over 200 delimited growing areas. A recent enhancement is the D.O.C.G. category (G stands for garantita) which includes some eighteen of Italy's best wines. These wines are evaluated by an official panel of tasters who guarantee their quality and authenticity. Many of Italy's best wines are discussed below in their respective regions.

The D.O.C. laws also regulate the use of certain terms associated with the producing zone and the finished wine. In some regions, where the wine comes from an established area long recognized for quality, the wine may be labelled Classico. One Italian wine term that always relates to quality is Riserva, or Reserve, identifying superior lots of wine that have been given additional aging prior to release. The minimum aging period for Riserva is fixed by law, depending on the wine or the region in which it is grown, which can be as little as a year or as long

as four years, for select red wines. Because wines sold as Riserva represent a small segment of the total production, they are usually rare and expensive.

One of the biggest recent revolutions in Italian wine-growing has been a new way of making red wines. Traditionally, most of the best Italian wines have been aged in large oak casks that have long since lost their oak extractives: they only serve to condition the wine as it ages. When put into smaller, new oak barrels, as is the practice in Bordeaux, the wine picks up plenty of oak flavors and undergoes a profound transformation over a period of several months. For many wine-growers, the resulting "new breed" of Italian wines is quite unlike anything experienced in this century.

Left: Harvest at Neirano, in the town of Mombaruzzo, Piedmont, Italy. The vintners appear to be happy because the weather held.

Above: Bruno and Marcello Ceretto, of the winemaking family that helped pave the way for a new style of Barolo.

Right: View in Piedmont near Treiso, confirming the alpine climate that influences the region.

However, there are strong traditions in Piedmont and Tuscany, and producers who oppose barrique aging say that the practice makes the wine merely taste of oak – not the original grape flavors nor the graceful maturity associated with bottle age. These same growers maintain that the original style of Barolos and Barbarescos contributed to their region's fame; why complicate this success with an entirely new style of wine? The battle is clearly not over, but one thing is certain: barrique aging, as a continuous process using new wood, has already profoundly influenced many Italian cellars and is not about to go away. It has already produced some spectacular new Barolos

and Barbarescos, and also some excellent Chardonnays that profit from new oak. It should be noted that all of these new barrique wines are fairly expensive, due to the cost of new oak barrels.

✿ Piedmont ✿

Piedmont (Piemonte) is a fusion of French cultural influences, a subalpine climate and a strong Italian heritage of wine-growing. Its location at the foot of the Alps is reflected in its name; it ranks as one of Italy's top wine producing areas. It is best known for its powerful red wines made from the Nebbiolo grape: two of the most famous are Barolo and Bar-

VALLE D'AOSTA

TRENTINO-ALTO ADIGE

FRIULI-VENEZIA
GIULIA

LOMBARDY

Trento

Piave

PIEDMONT

Milano

VENETO

Ticino

Oglio

Venice

Torino

Po

Tanaro

EMILIA ROMAGNA

Reno

Panaro

LIGURIA

Pisa

Arno

Florence

TUSCANY

MARCHE

UMBRIA

Tevere

I T A L Y

CORSICA

ABRUZZI

Rome

MOLISE

LATIUM

Ofanto

Bari

CAMPANIA

Naples

APULIA

Alghero

Sassari

BASILICATA

Tirso

Nuoro

Oristano

SARDINIA

CALABRIA

Cagliari

Reggio

Palermo

Messina

Mazara
del Vallo

SICILY

Agrigento

Siracusa

Valletta

Above left: Drawing a
cask sample in Barolo,
from the giant ovals
used in the region.
These big casks have a
minimal effect on the
wine, and long bottle
age is necessary.

Left: A Barbaresco
vineyard in winter,
showing the terraces
used in the area.

Above right: Angelo
Gaja, proponent of the
new barrique method in
Piedmont, samples
some grapes before
harvest.

0   100 miles

0   100 kilometers

baresco, both of which are grown in delimited areas in the Langhe Hills southeast of the city of Alba. When made in the traditional method, these wines are long-lived and need plenty of bottle age. More recent producers, in a style spearheaded by the Ceretto brothers, seek a lighter, more supple wine that may be enjoyed sooner. Other producers, most notably Angelo Gaja, age their wines via the barrique method, in French oak, with a radical change in style from

Left: The little town of Cormons, in Friuli, Italy.

Above: The center square in the town of Barolo in Piedmont, whose name now graces wine lists all over the world.

Right: Dolcetto grapes at the Castello di Neive, Piedmont, in a traditional wicker basket.

the older types of Barolos and Barbarescos. But whatever the approach, Barolo and Barbaresco rank as some of the world's truly greatest wines.

By law, Barolo must be aged a minimum of three years before being sold, two of them in cask. If the wine is at least five years old it may be sold as a Riserva. The rules are a bit less stringent for its neighbor Barbaresco – a lighter, more delicate wine: two years minimum aging, one in cask, and the wine qualifies as a Riserva

after four years. However, the quality standards of a particular producer make more of a difference in ultimate quality than the minimum official standards.

Good Producers: Barolo

Batasiolo, Bersano, Borgogno, Carretta, Cavallotto, Ceretto, Conterno, Contratto, Fontanafredda, Franco Fiorina, Bruno Giacosa, Granduca d'Asti, Marchesi di Barolo, Mascarello, Fratelli Oddero, Pio Cesare, Alfredo Prunotto, Renato Ratti, Francesco Rinaldi, Scavino, Terre del Barolo, Vietti.

Good Producers: Barbaresco

Luigi Bianco, Castello di Neive, Ceretto, Contratto, Giuseppe Cortese, Fontanafredda, Franco Fiorina, Angelo Gaja, Bruno Giacosa, Granduca d'Asti, Marchesi di Gresy, Fratelli Oddero, Pio Cesare, Produtorri del Barbaresco, Alfredo Prunotto, Renato Ratti, Francesco Rinaldi, Vietti.

Outstanding Piemontese wines are not limited to Barolo and Barbaresco. In the northeast, in the Novara and Vercelli

Hills, there are several outstanding wine regions that also grow Nebbiolo (locally called Spanna) sometimes mixed with Bonarda and Vespolina. The most celebrated wine of this area is Gattinara, grown near a village of the same name in a specific zone in the Vercelli Hills. Gattinara is softer and lighter than Barolo; in great vintages it has lovely complexity and smoothness. By law it may not be released until four years after the vintage, of which two years must be in wood. Equally distinctive, but rarer, is Ghemme.

Good Producers: Gattinara

Antoniolo, Brugo, Cantalupo (Collis Breclemae) Luigi Dessilani, Luigi Ferrando, Umberto Fiore, Travaglini, Antonio Vallana.

Good Producers: Ghemme

Canatalupo (Collis Breclemae), Agostino Brugo, Le Colline, Guido Ponti.

Many producers also grow varietal wines – Nebbiolo, Barbera and Dolcetto, which are native to the area. Nebbiolo, when grown in the delimited zone of Nebbiolo d'Alba, is a hardy D.O.C. wine that recalls Barolo but rarely achieves the same complexity. Barbera, a rugged variety, has an individual raspberry fruit combined with a characteristic high acidity. Both Barbera d'Alba and Barbera d'Asti are good examples of the grape, with the latter usually being a bit softer. Dolcetto wines have plenty of color and up-front fruit; they are often drunk young to capture their youthful vitality. In this respect they are often compared with Beaujolais. Some of the best examples come from Dolcetto di Diano d'Alba, in the heart of the district.

Piedmont has only recently become noted for its whites. In the past, most were grown from the Cortese grape, which tends to lack personality, but in the 1970s the delimited area of Gavi – particularly Gavi di Gavi, from the central part of the region – suddenly became very popular. On the whole, Gavis vary tremendously, from light, unassuming wines to racy, sensational mouthfuls. A rarity in Piedmont is Arneis, also called Roero Arneis, whose fresh, lively flavor suggests wildflowers. About twenty years ago, some Piedmont growers determined that their producing zone had many of the right conditions for growing Chardonnay. A number of new vineyards were planted in Chardonnay resulting in some spectacular barrique aged wines.

The area around Asti is noted for the sweet Asti Spumante, a sparkling wine made from the Moscato (Muscat) grape. Non-sparkling Muscats can find a potentially even bigger audience: the sweet, low-alcohol Moscato d'Asti is a real treat, as are some dessert Muscats made by a number of good producers in the Asti area.

Left: Kristof Tiefenbrunner, director of a famous estate in the Alto Adige, inspecting his vines. Here they are trained low, as opposed to the pergolas used further down in the valley.

Below left: The wines of the Friulian producer Ronco del Gnemiz, include many varietals unique to Friuli including Schioppettino, Verduzzo Friuliano and Tocai Friulano.

Right: A tractor brings in the harvest in Friuli; one of Italy's finest regions for white wines.

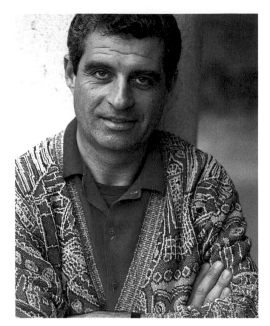

Gewürztraminer. All of these grapes give excellent results in the region.

Red grapes also flourish, although the wines tend to be lighter than they are further south. Trentino grows more of the familiar Bordeaux varieties, like Cabernet Franc, Cabernet Sauvignon and Merlot; these tend to have excellent fruit and are among the better values available from the district.

Good Producers:

Santa Margherita (and their superior proprietary white, Luna dei Feldi), Cavit (largest producer in Trentino), Josef Brigl, Alois Lageder, J. Tiefenbrunner, Pojer & Sandri, Kettmeir, J. Hofstatter, Schloss Rametz, Barone de Cles (Teroldego), Cantina Produttori Mezzocorona, Bollini.

❧ Trentino-Alto Adige ❧

Two associated provinces, Trentino and Alto Adige, grow exceptional wine all along the Adige River valley in the shadow of the Dolomites. The most northerly region in Italy, Trentino-Alto Adige borders Austria, and although it has been a permanent part of Italy since 1919, many of the wines still sport Germanic names. The wines are among the nation's best, and are particularly important on the export market.

In general, Trentino's climate is milder than Alto Adige, and red wines are easier to grow. But the alpine climate in the Alto Adige is especially favorable to high quality white wines, plus a few special reds. The vines may be grown on pergolas in the valley, or on trellises in terraced vineyards, depending on the soil and the grape variety. Because all of the wines typically show good acidity, sparkling wines are an important part of the region's total production.

In recent years, the most popular white grape variety in both Trentino and Alto Adige has been Pinot Grigio, owing to its fresh scent and delicious fruit flavor. Another is Chardonnay, along with Pinot Bianco (Pinot Blanc), which often recalls a good Burgundy – the difference is that these wines see little or no oak, and are lighter and crisper. In addition, there are Moscato or Muscat, Müller-Thurgau, Riesling Renano (the true Riesling of Germany), Sauvignon Blanc, Sylvaner and Traminer Aromatico, or

The sparkling wines of the area, or spumante, are among Italy's greatest. The cool climate of Trentino-Alto Adige provides ideal base wines for sparkling wine production, and the same grape varieties as the French Champagne district (Pinot Noir, Chardonnay) are grown – most of the bottles will be labelled "metodo classico" to show that the same process of bottle fermentation was used, although there are some Charmat process wines in the more basic quality categories.

Good Producers:

Ferrari, Cavit, Schloss Rametz.

Above left: Walter Filiputti, oenologist at the Abbazia di Rosazzo estate in Friuli, and consultant to many other famous properties in the region.

Below: View from Borgo Trerose, with the village of Montepulciano in the distance. This photo gives an idea of the hilly terrain in central Tuscany.

Right: Sangiovese grapes at Fattoria Le Casalte in Montepulciano. Sangiovese is the main grape in Tuscan red wines.

❋ Friuli-Venezia Giulia ❋

Friuli is the northeastern extreme of Italy, bordering Slovenia and Austria and home to some of Italy's most select wine districts. While many good reds are grown in Friuli, the whites are especially famous and in recent years have become popular on some of the top wine lists in Milan, Venice and Rome. But production in Friuli is lower than in surrounding wine regions, so the best wines tend to be relatively expensive.

The climate in Friuli is relatively cool, and in select hilly vineyards some of the top grape varieties give excellent results. Like its neighbor Alto Adige, Friuli sells most of its wines under their varietal names. The best known include Tocai, a

superb local variety, Pinot Grigio, Chardonnay, Pinot Bianco, Riesling Renano (Rhine Riesling), Müller-Thurgau, Sauvignon Blanc, Traminer and Verduzzo. The biggest D.O.C. zone is Grave del Friuli, west of the city of Udine and named for its porous gravelly soils. Two other important D.O.C.s lie further east in upland areas, and usually produce superior wines. They include Collio Goriziano or Collio, along the Slovenian border near the city of Gorizia; and Colli Orientali del Friuli, further north near the city of Cividale del Friuli.

Friuli's most illustrious white is probably the rare, expensive Picolit, a sweet white variety made only in limited quantities by a few growers. Picolit has a D.O.C. listing in the Colli Orientali area,

but may be grown in many other parts of Friuli, so quality is apt to vary but still remains high.

Good Producers:

EnoFriulia, Angoris, Jermann, Duca Badoglio, Marco & Livio Felluga, Ronco del Gnemiz, Abbazia di Rosazzo, Mario Schiopetto, Vigna dal Leon, Fratelli Furlan, Fratelli Pighin, and Casarsa.

❋ Tuscany ❋

Well known to tourists and wine lovers around the world, Tuscany is presently one of the most exciting areas in Italy for wine. The beautiful, rolling Tuscan hills are dotted with innovations in winegrowing, and Tuscan producers are stay-

Left: The official seal of the Consorzio del Marchio Storico Vino Chianti Classico: the black rooster, or gallo nero. In the US, this must be called marchio storico.

Below: Brightly painted red oak ovals used for aging Brunello di Montalcino, several years prior to bottling.

Above right: A Tuscan grower inspecting grapes which are hung up to dry for Vin Santo production. Although often compared to Sherry, Vin Santos vary dramatically from producer to producer.

Below right: Roberto Anselmi, of the famous Soave firm that bears his name, showing young vines that have been planted using a new technique.

ing in touch with the times as they market some impressive new vintages.

In a tradition dating back to the renaissance, Tuscany has long been associated with Chianti – the popular, easygoing red wine that seems so well-suited to Italian food. But in truth the region now has several dozen other delimited wine districts, and Chianti itself has undergone a major transformation in the last two decades. Basic Chianti is derived from the Sangiovese grape, with a proportion of Canaiolo for color and sweetness and a small amount of white grapes to lighten the blend. Chianti's better producers recently banded together and changed the rules for the grape blends. Since Chianti was essentially a light red wine that could also be produced with white grapes, the proportion of white grapes was reduced. The reds, meanwhile, are much improved and have solidly established Chianti's reputation for quality.

Officially, Chianti can be sold in the year following the vintage, but usually improves with another year in cask or in bottle. Better wines from superior lots, with a minimum of two years in cask and another in bottle, can be sold as Riserva. There are six approved areas for Chianti production; besides plain Chianti, they

include, from north to south, Chianti Colli Fiorentini, Chianti Rufina, Chianti Montalbano, Chianti Colli Aretini, Chianti Colline Pisane and Chianti Colli Senesi.

Good Producers:

Ruffino, Antinori, Frescobaldi (Chianti Rufina), Melini, Selvapiana, Lilliano.

The central or classic zone for Chianti, known as Chianti Classico, lies between the cities of Florence and Siena. The area includes the famous wine towns of Greve, Castellina, Gaole and Radda, and has many of the region's top producers. A guild, or consorzio, of Chianti Classico growers was established in 1924 to promote the region's wines and maintain high quality standards. The Consorzio del Marchio Storico Chianti Classico identified its members with its traditional emblem, a black rooster seal originally known as the Gallo Nero – now known as the Marchio Storico, or historic emblem, after a lawsuit by the Gallo Winery of California challenged the use of this name. Chianti Classico

Above: The lovely Umbrian countryside, as seen from the estate of Borgo Trerose.

Above right: Christiana Dubili, a producer from Palazzone in Central Italy.

Riserva Sergio Zenato

AMARONE 1980

COLORE: ROSSO RUBINO
SAPORE: MOLTO CORPOSO, INTENSO, ELEGANTE ED ASCIUTTO
PROFUMO: MOLTO SPEZIATO DA FRUTTA SECCA (PRUGNA) DOVUTO ALL'INVECCHIAMENTO IN PICCOLI BOTTI PER 18/24 MESI.

AMARONE 1983

COLORE: ROSSO RUBINO
SAPORE: RETROGUSTO AMAROGNOLO, ALCOLICITÀ MORBIDA E CALDA
PROFUMO: FRUTTATO CON GUSTO DA FRUTTA SECCA, BUONA TOSTATURA, INVECCHIATO IN BOTTI DI LEGNO PER 18/24 MESI.

AMARONE 1985

COLORE: ROSSO RUBINO CARICO
SAPORE: PIENO, MAESTOSO, DI GRANDE SPESSORE
PROFUMO: ETEREO, INTENSO E FINE, DA GRANDE VINO INVECCHIATO IN BOTTI PER 16/18 MESI.

has somewhat more stringent standards for aging than straight Chianti. Itmay be aged and sold after two years, but if given two years of wood aging and another in bottle, it can be labelled Riserva.

Good Producers:

Marchesi Antinori, Ruffino Riserva Ducale, Castello di Fonterutoli (Mazzei), Isole e Olena, Badia a Coltibuono, Castellare, Monsanto, Castello del Volpaia, Monte Vertine, Fattoria di Felsina (Berardenga), Villa Cerna (Cecchi).

Tuscany has also built much of its reputation on the select, rare wines of Brunello di Montalcino, grown from a clone of Sangiovese around the little town of Montalcino in central Tuscany. Virtually unknown outside the area before the 1970s, Brunello's fame is now world-wide, and the wines fetch high prices in the trade. Made from Brunello, which is a clone of Sangiovese, Brunello di Montalcino is kept in wood and in bottle longer than Chianti and takes longer

to mature. But the associated Rosso di Montalcino, grown in vintages when Brunello is not generally declared, have much of the same character for a lot less money.

Good Producers:

Fattoria di Barbi (Colombini), Biondi-Santi, Altesino, Castello Banfi, Silvio Nardi, Val di Suga, Tenuta Argiano, Emilio Costanti.

A third Tuscan red, Vino Nobile di Montepulciano, potentially relates to some of the region's best wines. But quality of this "noble" wine has not always been consistent among certain producers. It is grown in a delimited zone around the little town of Montepulciano, and has elements in common with Chianti and Brunello but usually seems smoother and a bit fruitier.

Carmignano, a Tuscan red famous for centuries but relatively late to be ranked as a D.O.C., is another delicious wine whose fame in large part relates to its

major producer, Count Ugo Bonnacosi. This dynamic winemaking family has also experimented with French grapes for their proprietary red Ghiaie della Furba, and their excellent white wine made from Chardonnay.

Tuscany was one of the original areas where the D.O.C. laws did not always apply to superior quality. Perhaps the best example is Sassicaia, a superb Cabernet-based wine produced by the Marchesi Incisa della Rochetta at his estate near Livorno; since it did not conform to the laws, it could only be sold as vino da tavola. The same applied to Marchesi Antinori's lovely Tignanello, a San-giovese/Cabernet blend that helped launch a whole new generation of Tuscan wines.

Tuscan whites tended to be eclipsed by the reds, until the advent of Galestro added to supply and improved winemaking methods made the wines more stable for export. One of the best traditional whites is the Vernaccia di San Gimignano, a fresh-tasting wine grown around the picturesque village of San

Left: Two giants of the Campania district: Carlo and Antonio Mastroberardino, who make Taurasi and Fiano d'Avellino.

Right: De Bartoli, one of the finest producers of Marsala, offers a drier version called Josephine Doré.

Gimignano in central Tuscany. Newer methods of vinification have made it stable, and its fresh melony flavor makes it an ideal accompaniment with food.

❧ Veneto ❧

Veneto, with its gateway city of Venice on the Adriatic, is Italy's most productive vineyard area. The wines are extremely well known on the export market because the key producers have been supplying their wines for decades; despite a persistent problem of overproduction, there is an especially rich variety of wines from the Veneto area.

Probably the three best known wine names from Veneto are Soave, Valpolicella and Bardolino, all grown around the city of Verona in the western section of the province. Soave relies predominantly on the Garganega grape; the two reds are made from a blend of Corvina, Negrara, and Molinara. If grown in the central and best portion of their respective districts, they may be called Classico; if their alcohol is at least one percent higher than the minimum, they may be labelled Superiore. Since they share the same grape varieties, Valpolicella and Bar-dolino are quite similar, but the latter is usually a lighter, less interesting wine.

One of Veneto's potentially best whites is Bianco di Custoza, grown in the area between Lake Garda and Lombardy and produced from a blend of Trebbiano, Tocai and Garganega. Breganze, now a D.O.C. describing an area north of Vicenza, is equally celebrated for its fresh, lively white wines.

Good Producers:

Allegrini, Bertani (and their proprietary brand, Catullo), Fratelli Bolla, Lamberti, Santa Margherita, Fratelli Zenato, Maculan (Breganze), Masi, Anselmi, Santa Sofia, Tommasi, Fratelli Tedeschi, Sartori.

The specialty of many Valpolicella producers is Amarone (full name: Recioto della Valpolicella Amarone), made from selected grape bunches that have been set aside to dry for about two weeks prior to vinification. Because of the evaporation, Amarones are rich and concentrated, and high in alcohol (usually over 14%). They are fairly expensive and need time in bottle to age, but are among the best red wines of Italy.

Good Producers:

Masi, Bolla (much improved lately), Allegrini, Santa Sofia, Bertani, Zenato, Le Ragose, Giuseppe Quintarelli, Tommasi, Sartori, Serego Alighieri.

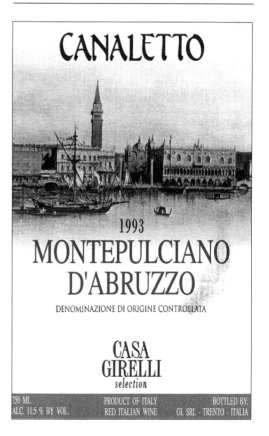

CANALETTO

1993

MONTEPULCIANO D'ABRUZZO

DENOMINAZIONE DI ORIGINE CONTROLLATA

CASA GIRELLI
selection

750 ML
ALC. 11.5 % BY VOL.

PRODUCT OF ITALY
RED ITALIAN WINE

BOTTLED BY:
GL SRL - TRENTO - ITALIA

white and rosés grown in a delimited zone near the lower slopes of Mount Vesuvius (Vesuvio), which itself became a D.O.C. in 1983 and relates to more ordinary grades. All three wines are usually quite sound, and Mastroberardino is the best known producer.

The Mastroberardinos are among the producers of the region's best red wine, Taurasi, grown from the Aglianico grape in the hilly area northeast of Naples, near the little town of Avellino. Now officially rated D.O.C.G., Taurasi is a select wine by any standards; robust but smooth, and capable of brilliance with aging: it may be sold as Riserva if over 4 years old.

There are two select D.O.C. white Campanian wines from this area: Greco di Tufo, grown from the venerable Greco variety near the little town of Avellino; and the even finer Fiano di Avellino, which are wonderful wines with the regional cuisine that includes seafood specialties.

Two small islands near the Gulf of Naples have their own D.O.C. listings: Capri, applying to adequate reds and better whites grown in a rather small area; and Ischia, the larger and more important of the two, with occasionally excellent reds (the best are called Per e Palummo) and white wines.

❧ Umbria ❧

Umbria's most famous white wine is Orvieto, produced from a blend of Trebbiano, Grechetto and Malvasia and grown around a city of the same name in a wide variety of styles. The most popular form is the dry or secco version, but because some consumers like a fruitier wine, there is a semi-dry or amabile version as well, which is essentially the same wine with a small amount of residual sweetness.

Good Producers:

Vaselli, Bigi, Antinori, Ruffino.

In the Torgiano area the illustrious Lungarotti family have been involved in a major effort to upgrade the local wines and also make some original contributions of their own. Their Torgiano red

and white is consistently good, but the Rubesco Riserva, a proprietary label, is even better. The Lungarottis were among the first to plant Chardonnay, Sauvignon Blanc and Gewürztraminer in the area two decades ago, and their San Giorgio, an original Sangiovese/Cabernet blend, is a sensational wine by any standard.

❧ Campania ❧

Campania, with its uncommonly beautiful coastline and its rich history, is another perfect spot for vineyards. The region has a long heritage of wine-growing, dating back to ancient Greece.

The Naples region is probably best known for Lacryma Christi, "Christ's Tears," which relates to an ancient legend in which Jesus' tears were transformed into wine. Although the legend is old, it took almost forever for the wine to become a D.O.C.; it now applies to red,

❧ Abruzzo ❧

The Abruzzi, as the hills of Abruzzo are called, are rugged and isolated; the highest peaks of the Apennines are snow capped even in summer. But in select low lying areas north and south of the city of Chieti, two of Italy's most consistent and affordable wines are grown: the white Trebbiano d'Abruzzo, and the superior red Montepulciano d'Abruzzo, both named for the informing varieties and both rated D.O.C. In particular, Montepulciano d'Abruzzo can be a magnificent wine – fruity when young, and smooth and velvety when aged. Occasionally a vecchio version may be released when over two years old.

Good Producers:

Casal Thaulero, Illuminati, Barone Cornacchia, Dario d'Angelo, Bruno Nicodemi, Ponti, and Edouardo Valentini.

✿ Apulia ✿

Apulia, or Puglia, is the "heel" of the Italian boot – an extremely prolific wine district and a valuable source of rich, robust red wine used traditionally for blending in the northern districts. In recent years improvements in viticulture and tighter controls have diminished this practice, and now many Apulian wines are becoming famous on their own merits. The region extends over a very large area, extending from the city of Foggia in the north down to the port city of Taranto to the south.

There are some 23 wine districts entitled to D.O.C. in Apulia, but only a few of them are familiar outside the region and some of the best wines do not even qualify for D.O.C. A prime example is Torre Quarto, grown by the Cirillo-Farrusi estate near Cerignola, an excellent red wine made from a blend of Malbec and Negroamaro vinified in the Bordeaux style. Another is Favonio, grown by the Simonini estate, whose Chardonnays and Cabernet Francs are often exceptional. The best wines of the Salento area, grown mostly from Negroamaro, also do not carry a D.O.C. Some

of them are late harvested wines, produced by an ancient method of drying the grapes prior to vinification. Good examples are the Negrino of De Castris and the Patriglione of Dr. Cosimo Taurino.

The best known Apulian D.O.C. areas include Castel del Monte, describing red, white and rosés grown southwest of the city of Bari. The reds, made from Uva di Troia and Montepulciano, are particularly fine. Primitivo, a robust red variety grown extensively in southern Apulia, may be related to California's Zinfandel – except that the rich red wines of this area are usually rather different. Squinzano, a D.O.C. describing rich red wines made from Negroamaro grown near the town of Squinzano, used to be a generic term for the robust reds of this area. Now one of the best D.O.C.s is Salice Salentino, a superior red produced from Negroamaro in a delimited area near the town of Lecce.

Good Producers:

Rivera (Castel del Monte), Cirillo-Farussi, Dr. Cosimo Taurino (Salice Salentino), de Castris, Simonini (Favonio).

✿ Sicily ✿

More than in most other Italian wine regions, Sicily suffers from recurrent drought in summer, and the hot climate traditionally limited the selection of wine grapes to those that could endure it. Thus Sicily's most famous wine, Marsala, is a fortified wine produced much as it was over two hundred years ago, when English entrepreneur John Woodhouse first perfected the formula. But new vineyards are radically changing the face of the Sicilian wine industry.

A few Sicilian grapes are indigenous to the island. The most important are the white Catarrato and Inzolia, which are used in Marsala production as well as for other whites; and the reds Nerello Mascalese and Perricone. In some places vestigial Greek varieties, such as Malvasia and Moscato (Muscat), recall a long tradition of sweet wine production. But the real excitement dates back only a few years, when French varieties like Cabernet Sauvignon and Sauvignon Blanc were first planted in some of the cooler areas of the island and gave astonishingly good results.

Grown in a delimited zone west of the

capital city of Palermo, Marsala is ideally set up for fortified wine production. Marsala is very important in la cucina italiana – Italian cooking. The drier types are a necessary ingredient to many dishes, and the sweeter types are superb with desserts. All of the wines have a family resemblance, a faint caramel flavor resulting from the mosto cotto – reduced grape must that is a necessary stage in Marsala production. This difference in flavor sets Marsala apart from Sherry, and highlights its importance as a unique product of Italy.

A D.O.C. wine for over twenty years, Marsala has several quality grades. The most basic wines, which go into commercial blends, are graded fine: they must be aged at least one year and must have a minimum alcoholic content of 17%. Those graded superiore must reach a minimum strength of 18% and be aged at least two years before being sold. The unique grade of vergine applies to dry Marsalas that have been aged at least five years and are unblended with older wines, through the solera system that is standard method of production in most regions involved with fortified wine production. The best Marsalas are aged for

at least ten years, and may be labelled *Riserva or Stravecchio.*

A common white wine in the Palermo region is Alcamo Bianco, grown in a wide area in western Sicily but with no great claim to fame; except the wines of Corvo, from the Duca di Salaparuta estate east of Palermo, which have become one of the great Italian success stories. There is a Corvo red as well, and their crowning achievement is the Palumbo Platino series, a super-premium blend of selected wines, aged in barrique and given additional bottle age prior to release.

An innovative producer in Sicily is Conte Lucio Tasca d'Almerita, proprietor

f the Regaleali estate southeast of Palermo, who works with traditional varietals as well as with newer varieties like Cabernet Sauvignon, Chardonnay and Sauvignon Blanc. The Donna Fugata estate in Benice, central Sicily is another noted producer of table wines. The surroundings of Mount Etna, Italy's most active volcano, are excellent for vineyards and Etna Rosso was one of the first Sicilian wines designated as DOC.

Sweet fortified wines have always been a Sicilian specialty. Two of the best are the Malvasia di Lipari, grown on the island of Lipari, and the Moscato di Pantelleria, also an island vineyard.

Left: Regaleali, owned by the Tasca d'Almerita family in Sicily, uses reservoirs to cope with the frequent droughts in the region.

Right: A part of the Regaleali estate in Sicily.

PORTUGAL

Portugal has undergone a winemaking transformation in the past twenty years, as tastes and production changed from mostly fortified wines, like Port and Madeira, to a greater proportion of table wines. From the cool, foggy north all the way down to the dry, sunny Algarve area, Portugal affords opportunities for all types of vineyards. While their grapes and production methods may vary according to the climate and the soil, their winemakers draw from centuries of experience, and also a long, established friendship with England that dates back over five hundred years.

Wine-growing in Portugal is controlled by the National Wine Institute in Lisbon, which sets official standards for production and regulates the number of vineyards that may be planted in a particular area (Denomiação de Origem). Portugal has many delimited wine areas under Denomiação de Origem, and more are expected to follow as growers modernize their cellars and vineyards. In the north, is the traditional Vinho Verde area, the producing zone for the "green wines," known to the many tourists who enjoy drinking them. Although most of the Vinho Verdes are white, there are reds as well; all with the same characteristic acidity that reflects their cool growing area.

The region of Bairrada near Oporto was recently delimited for red table wines, and they are now becoming quite popular. In general the name relates to smooth, fruity reds, and the older, better wines sometimes take on the name "Garrafeira," meaning private reserve, which spends a minimum of two years in cask and one in bottle.

In the past, many of Portugal's sweet, cheap rosés came from the north central zone, and were sold under a brand name without any indication of origin. As tastes became more sophisticated, and demand for dry table wines grew, growers changed their production methods and now a much wider variety of wine types is offered.

The Port wine region has been well identified for some three centuries, but in addition to the production of Port, some of the growers in the Alto Douro have seen the possibilities for red table wine, using many of the same grapes, and a whole new generation of table wines has now emerged. A few growers have experimented with French varieties like Cabernet Sauvignon and are garnering excellent results. These wines are of course not sold as Port, and are bottled in totally different bottles with their own names, but the climatic advantage that Port enjoys is clearly reflected in their quality. Perhaps the best known example is the Barca Velha from Ferreira ("Ferreirinha"), but there are several others.

Good Producers:

Valle Pradinhos, Quinta da Pacheca, Tinto de Anfora, Quinta do Corval, Quinta do Cotto.

Further south, around the city of Viseu, is a venerable old table wine producing zone: Dão. The appellation is used for red, white and rosés, but the reds are the best known and most representative portion of the production.

Good Producers:

Grao Vasco, Terras Altas, Quinta da Insua.

No discussion of Portuguese reds would be complete without Periquita, the informing grape of the Alentejo district and also the trade name of a popular red on the export market, produced by Jose Maria da Fonseca. This excellent wine, and also the Quinta da Bacalhoa owned by Joao Pires, typifies the improvements

made by Portuguese table wine producers during the last two decades.

Lisbon can claim one of the finest sweet dessert wines in the world, the Moscatel de Setúbal, grown in a small area near the bay of Lisbon. Made from the sweet Moscatel grape, the wine is light-amber, lusciously sweet and takes on delectable nuances with age.

❧ Port ❧

Port – specifically, the unique product of the Alto Douro district in northern Portugal – is one of the world's noblest wines. Like Sherry, Port is a fortified wine, to which brandy is added to stop fermentation in its initial stages; but unlike Sherry, which has a mature nutty flavor, Port tends to taste more like fresh grapes.

Most Port wine is red, and it tends to be rather sweet; there is also some white Port grown, which is popular in Europe, but it has yet to take hold so far in the U.S. All Port wine is subject to the controls of the Instituto do Vinho do Porto, which oversees standards for production and affixes a seal on each bottle stating that it is the genuine product of the Port region in Portugal. This is necessary because a lot of "port" is grown in other countries, like Australia and the U.S., which although they may be excellent wines in their own right, do not always taste like the Portuguese product.

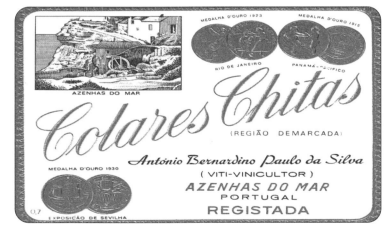

There are actually two centers of the Port wine trade. The economic center is the city of Oporto, at the mouth of the Douro River, which lends its name to its famous wine. The Port shippers have their headquarters or lodges here, and also in the adjacent town of Vila Nova de Gaia. The second center is the Alto Douro growing district, some 120 km upstream, which is the only area where grapes for Port wine may be grown. A rugged and uncommonly beautiful area, the exact boundaries of the Alto Douro district were officially delimited over 200 years ago by the Marques de Pombal, a visionary who wanted to insure that the quality and authenticity of Port would never be compromised.

The Douro River draws its source in Spain, and much of its length is ideal for vineyards. But only in the central part, around the towns of Pinhão and Regua, is the altitude, soil and exposure right for the grapes used for Port. There, in a process completed over many centuries, little terraces have been carved and blasted out of the hillsides so that vines could be planted.

The first step in Port production is a selection of the right grapes: not just one variety alone, but several, planted according to soil type, which will blend together and create the right flavor combinations. The backbone of Port is the Touriga Nacional, a sweet, flavorful grape ideally suited to the Alto Douro. Touriga is one of five principal varieties used in the blends: others include Touriga Francesca, Tinta Cão, Tinta Barroca and Tinta Roriz; white Port is produced from Rabigato, Gouveio, Viosinho, Códega or Malvasia Fina.

At harvest time, the grapes are gathered in the vineyards and brought to a press house for crushing. For centuries, the custom in the Alto Douro has been to crush grapes by treading with the feet. Although this practice has now almost entirely been replaced by machinery, foot treading is still used for the best wines, and it does have certain advantages. As performed in the traditional concrete vats, foot treading is done over a period of several days, and the steady, gentle weight of the human foot is ideal for the crushing process. But because of high labor costs, this romantic old method has given way to modern stainless steel rotary fermenters.

Fermentation usually follows swiftly after crushing. But soon after it starts, a specific quantity of neutral spirits is added to the wine, which brings it up to about 20% alcohol by volume. This is enough to stop further fermentation, and the resulting wine still has the delicious ripe flavor of fresh crushed grapes. The wines spend their first few months in the Alto Douro, then they are brought downstream to Vila Nova de Gaia for blending and aging. They are normally not aged in the Douro, because the hot summers there are not conducive to long-term aging.

There are two groups of Port: ruby and tawny. Ruby, named for its rich ruby color, is usually rather sweet; tawny is lighter and drier, and tends to have an amber color. The differences relate to the processing: ruby is made with a minimum of wood aging, while tawnies spend some time in cask, thereby acquiring a characteristic tawny color.

These two groups not only describe the Port spectrum, but define the most basic offerings. Regular ruby and tawny Port is the entry level for many shippers, and these wines are not sold with any indication of vintage. The word "vintage" has a different meaning in Port wine, because only certain years produce wines with qualities that allow them to be sold with an indication of vintage. Legally, authentic Vintage Port is a selection of the best lots of ruby in a particular vintage, which must be aged a maximum of two years in cask prior to being bottled. A vintage is "declared" by a shipper when the quality of these special lots is judged superior, but depending on the firm's standards, a shipper may only declare a vintage a few times a decade.

Left: Wicker hods used for transporting grapes in the Alto Douro region in Portugal.

Right: General view of terraced vineyards in the Port district, Alto Douro.

Thus Vintage Port is rare and quite expensive; it is a massive wine requiring at least ten years of age in bottle to really show its qualities.

Most Vintage Port is marketed with the name of the shipper. In recent years a second type of Vintage Port has been released by some shippers, which is sold with the name of the informing vineyard or quinta. These "vintage quintas" are actually Vintage Ports produced in years not generally declared as a vintage, and are usually lighter and less expensive than the main label, but may still be extraordinary. Their quality is often superior to Vintage Ports from less conscientious producers. Better examples include the Quinta Malvedos of Graham, Quinta da Vargellas from Taylor, Quinta da Cavadinha of Warre's, Quinta do Bomfim of Dow, Quinta do Tua of Cockburn, Quinta do Vesuvio, Quinta da Romaneira and the Quinta do Crasto.

Despite all of its great fame, Vintage Port only makes up about 2 to 3% of the total production of Port. Besides the workhorse grades of ruby and tawny, there are other important types of Port. Two of the most popular ruby types are the "vintage character" Ports, which are finer versions of ruby made from blends averaging from 4 to 5 years; and Late-bottled vintage Ports. Unlike Vintage Port, Late-bottled vintage (LBV) Ports are bottled 4 - 6 years after the vintage, tend to be lighter and do not throw down as much sediment as they mature. They are also much less expensive and can be produced in years when Vintage Ports are not generally declared by shippers.

Tawny Ports are lighter and drier than rubies, and many Port drinkers – particularly Europeans – prefer them for this reason. Basic tawny is produced from selected lots of lighter, drier wines that have spent longer in cask and have undergone a slight oxidation. These Ports are available in 10-year, 20-year, 30-year and 40-year old blends. The older the age of these wines is a general indication of quality.

Because of England's traditional role in the Port wine trade, many Port shippers have English names and English directors. The best known include Taylor/Fladgate, Fonseca, Graham, Warre's, Dow (Silva & Cossens), Croft, Cockburn, Smith/Woodhouse, Sandeman, Offley/Forrester, Robertson, Churchill, Delaforce and the famous single Quinta do Noval. Portuguese-controlled houses include Niepoort, Ferreira, Cálem, Ramos-Pinto, Rozes, Borges, Royal, Burmester, Kopke and Feist.

The best Port vintages of the past few decades have been 1945, 1948, 1955, 1960, 1963, 1966, 1970, 1975, 1977, 1980, 1982, 1983, 1985, 1991, 1992 and 1994. Vintage quintas can be produced in many good vintages, but are not normally declared in the same years as Vintage Port.

❧ Madeira ❧

The island of Madeira lies out in the Atlantic Ocean about 1,000 km (600 mi.) off the coast of Africa, and is actually the top of an enormous volcano that rises up from the bottom of the ocean. A ruggedly beautiful island, Madeira has been under Portuguese control since 1409, and wine has been grown there for over five hundred years.

Madeira's first wines were thin, sour and very mediocre. Early winemakers experimented by adding brandy to the wines to strengthen them for the sea voyage, which helped; but after months at sea, it was discovered that the constant heat and motion aboard ship actually improved the wines, and thus Madeira became a regular part of a ship's cargo during colonial times. Any other wine would have spoiled, but Madeira's endurance to tropical heat soon became legendary.

The heat and motion of the long ocean voyage in the tropics gave Madeira its special flavor; but the results were often inconsistent. To regulate production before the wines left the island, Madeira shippers developed the estufa system in the early nineteenth century, whereby the young wines are put into heated hot-water ovens for a period of several months, thereby developing the required flavor and color.

Madeira's labels identify the degree of sweetness as well as the grape, some of which are Sercial, Verdelho and Rainwater. The sweeter Madeiras are generally the most representative, because the wine's fine, caramel flavor is best offset by some sweetness. Bual, or Boal, is usually rather sweet but has a delectable texture and aroma that sets it apart. The sweetest and "fattest" of all the Madeiras is Malmsey, relating to an English mispronunciation of Malvasia – a native Mediterranean grape that thrives in Madeira's climate. Malmsey is usually very sweet, and its characteristic low acidity gives it additional roundness and body. The production of most Madeira is standardized by the solera system – a constant blending process through tiers of casks.

Vintages work differently in Madeira

Decanting Vintage Port the elegant way: using a crystal decanter and a silver funnel, with a strainer in the middle to catch the sediment.

than for Port. While there is of course a vintage each year on the island, producers regularly set aside a small portion of their best production for additional aging. This continues for another ten years in cask and the remainder in large demijohns, before being decanted into regular bottles. Legally today, a vintage Madeira may not be sold before it is twenty-five years old, and even then it can be expected to improve indefinitely in bottle. These wines are totally unlike regular Madeira; in fact, they are unlike almost any other wine. Regardless of the grape variety, vintage Madeiras are packed with flavor, and have a special intensity. Unfortunately they are also extremely rare and expensive.

Two-thirds of the entire production of Madeira is in the hands of the British-controlled Madeira Wine Company, which owns several of the best-known labels and conforms to very high quality standards. Traditional names like Cossart/Gordon, Leacock, Miles (formerly Rutherford & Miles), Blandy's, Welsh Brothers, and Henriques & Henriques are all labels associated with the British Madeira Wine Company. There may be some minor differences between the labels, but the wines are all vinified at the same source. (The familiar Justino's label is independent.)

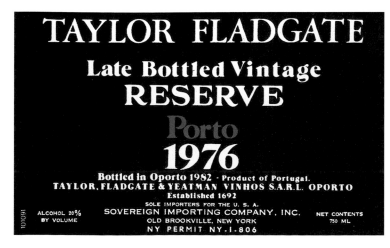

SPAIN

Wine-growing in Spain is justifiably part of the national pride, and relates to a tradition dating back thousands of years. Much of the land on the Iberian Peninsula is perfect for vineyards and olive groves, and over three million acres are now under vines. But because of the dry climate, and the fact that irrigation is not allowed in the wine districts, Spain's total production is well below Italy and France. Still, it is the third largest in the world.

A nation with a fine culinary heritage tends to have a great winemaking heritage as well, and Spain is no exception. In the case of her most famous export, Sherry, winemaking has been well established there since medieval times. The trend to upgrade table wine production in Spain has been more recent, but since Spain and Portugal's entry into the European Common Market in 1986 this has been occurring at a rapid pace. Dozens of excellent new producers are now entering the market. These are exciting times for Spanish winegrowers.

Each of the better wine districts has been delimited and entitled to its own appellation, known as the Denominación de Origen, which establishes regional boundaries, authorizes specific grape varieties and sets limits on yields. There are now over thirty approved wine dis-

Left: Miguel Torres, whose family helped change the history of Spanish wines, at the door of his cellars.

Right: The famous cellars of Lopez de Heredia, a landmark in the Rioja area. Their older reservas are especially celebrated.

Left: A Rueda winemaker checks his vines, which are deliberately pruned low.

Right: The famous castle of Peñafiel, Ribera del Duero, looks over an area that is becoming increasingly noted for its wines.

Below: Mariano Garcia, the winemaker for the famous winery Vega Sicilia, in springtime garb.

tricts throughout the country; the most famous of these, Rioja and Sherry, were the first to be delimited, in 1926 and 1933 respectively, but since the 1970s the ranks have swelled with other wine districts that have finally been able to modernize their vineyards and cellars, and profit from the recent economic boom taking place in Spain.

Sherry is the most famous fortified wine of Andalucia (Andalusia), along with the sweet Málaga grown in a city of that name to the east; but Montilla-Moriles, also a part of Andalucia, is another traditional wine name in the region and was celebrated for its fortified wines not long after Sherry made its reputation. Montillas can be excellent and are usually excellent values as they are much less expensive than Sherry.

Since the death of dictator Generalissimo Franco in 1975, the region of Catalonia has seen a boom in wine-growing – first with a flood of bottle-fermented sparkling wines, from the areas of Villafranca del Pénedes and San Sadurni de Noya, then with an exciting series of table wines made from new varieties not previously grown in the region, which proved to be especially well-suited to the Catalonian climate. Among the biggest sparkling wine producers, Codorniu saw the importance of exports very early, but their rival Freixenet soon caught up with them and jointly the Catalonian sparkling wine producers were shipping over a million cases a year to the U.S. market by the early 1980s.

The famous firm Miguel Torres s.a., of Villafranca del Pénedes, initially established their reputation on traditional Catalonian wines, but in the 1970s showed that many new grape varieties were well-suited to the region's exceptional climate. The present director, Miguel Torres, is credited with being

Left: Bodegas Muga is a popular producer in the area in Rioja.

Right: La Guardia, a pretty village with an exceptional location in the Rioja Alavesa district.

among the first to plant Cabernet Sauvignon, Merlot, Cabernet Franc and Chardonnay in the cooler uplands, and these are now familiar to winelovers all over the world. Similarly, the firms Jean Léon and René Barbier also make good examples of these varieties.

Nor have other wine-growing regions in Spain been caught napping. A particularly dynamic area today is the province of Castille-Léon, especially along the Duero River near the city of Valladolid, where the recent approval of two areas, Rueda (white) and Ribera del Duero (red), led to a surge in quality wine-growing during the past decade. One of Spain's very greatest (and most expensive) wines is Vega Sicilia, grown just outside Valladolid; they now have a rival in Pesquera, a more recent endeavor of Ale-

jandro Fernandez, who uses grape varieties native to France and ages his wines in French oak. Dozens of other cellars are cropping up in this area; it is clearly a region to watch closely.

Further south, the province of La Mancha is mostly suited to bulk wine production, but there are some good estates that bottle under their own name. Their wines are usually sound and quite inexpensive. In general, because of the hot, dry summers, the red wines are superior to the whites, and very often the rosé (rosado) wines are a preferred choice.

Until recently, Spanish white wines have not kept pace with the reds. This totally changed with the advent of some new, exciting white wines from Galicia in the northwest. The racy, clean Albarinos from this area, particularly those from

Rias Baixas, are unlike most other Spanish whites and are a sensational accompaniment to the area's delicious seafood.

Rioja

In terms of volume, exports and traditional importance, the areas of Rioja and Sherry are still the two most famous wine districts in Spain. Today, based on the wine's familiarity and the number of wineries involved, Rioja is surging ahead in popularity. Its soft, supple red wines are ideal with many foods; the whites are better than ever, and a few producers are making rosés that can compete with the world's best.

The name Rioja is actually a contraction of Rio Oja, the river that runs through the little town of Haro in the

center of the district. Rioja includes three distinct regions. The central and highest region is Rioja Alta, with the coolest climates and the lightest soils. The middle region is Rioja Alavesa, which is progressively warmer, and the lower region is Rioja Baja, with correspondingly coarser soils and a harsher climate. The differences in each region determine which grape varieties get planted: Rioja Alta is almost exclusively planted in Tempranillo, while Rioja Alavesa has more Mazuelo and Rioja Baja has more Garnacha, in addition to Tempranillo. Most red Rioja is a blend of all these grapes, but the most important is Tempranillo, which gives the wine its characteristic flavor and finesse.

White Rioja, which used to be a distant second to the reds in popularity, is now much improved. The better whites are made either exclusively or largely from Viura, and are vinified in chilled stainless steel tanks to preserve the fresh flavor of the grapes.

The blends and vinification methods in Rioja are quite similar to Bordeaux, and the similarity is no accident. Many Bordeaux winemakers came to Rioja originally in the 1880s to flee the phylloxera, and brought with them many of their proven techniques. One of these is extensive wood aging in oak casks, which rounds out the flavor but also adds a strong distinctive flavor of oak to the Rioja wine.

Rioja sold with an indication of vintage is known as Crianza; better grades, which are made from selected lots bearing a minimum of two years aging in cask and three in bottle, are called Reserva, and if aged for three years in cask and four in bottle, Gran Reserva.

Good Producers:

Marqués de Riscal, Marqués de Cáceres, Bodegas Olarra, Siglo, Compania Vinicola del Norte de España (C.U.N.E.), López de Heredia, Bodegas Muga, La Rioja Alta (Vina Ardanza), Marqués de Murietta, and Bodegas Bilbainas (Vina Pomal).

Above: Using eggs for the fining process at Bodegas Muga, Rioja. Only the whites are used to clarify the wines.

Left: Bodegas Marqués de Cáceres, owned by the Forner family, is a leading Rioja producer.

Right: A picker holds up some ripe Palomino grapes in Jerez de la Frontera, Spain. This grape is responsible for all the best Sherries.

Left: View of Bodega Emilio Lustau, one of the finest Sherry producers, showing the tiered casks used for the solera system.

Below left: Miguel Valdespino, of the bodega that bears his name, pouring a sample of Sherry in the traditional method using a real "cask thief."

Right: Harvey's of Bristol uses these barrels at their bodegas in Jerez.

Sherry

Numerous references to "sack" in Shakespeare's plays stand testament to Sherry's popularity in medieval Britain, a trend that continues to this day. Sherry's name actually stems from the English mispronunciation of Jerez de la Frontera, the seaport city where the wine is sold, and after installing themselves rather early in Jerez, English wine merchants did a thriving business with Sherry over the next several hundred years.

The principal grape in the Sherry district is Palomino, which constitutes over 90% of all the grapes in the area. A small quantity of Pedro Ximénez grapes are grown as a supplement, for the sweeter grades of Sherry. There is one segment of the Sherry district, immediately adjacent

to the seaport town of San Lúcar de Barrameda, where the vineyards are quite close to the ocean and produce a special, dry tangy wine with a character all its own. This is the famous Manzanilla, usually the lightest, driest and most aromatic of all Sherries.

The production of Sherry still involves a time-honored tradition of foot crushing, gently preparing the grape must for its eventual transformation into wine. The timing of fortification is important: when brandy is added to the must before little or any fermentation takes place, the result will be a sweet Sherry; if it is added after the wine ferments, the resulting wine will stay dry. But this is only a preliminary step in defining the various grades of Sherry.

The cellar is where the mysteries of Sherry occur. For reasons that are only partly understood, a particular yeast called "flor" (technically called Mycodermi vini) forms a protective film on selected casks of Sherry, protects it from oxidation and rounds out the flavor. The amazing thing about this yeast is its selectivity; not all casks will develop it, and no two casks are alike.

Casks that mature successfully with the flor yeast will be blended for the lightest grades of Sherry, known as Fino. Light Fino Sherries are among the driest and finest fortified wines available; served chilled, they are like a light, refreshing white wine and in fact are more substantial than most. Fuller bodied wines, with less of the flor characteristic, may be sold as Amontillado. Commercial grades of Amontillado may be blends of less successful Finos with heavier Sherries, but a good Amontillado represents a splendid all-purpose apéritif wine, golden brown, with a nutty flavor and a lovely aromatic bouquet.

Casks that develop no flor yeast are used for blends of Oloroso, which is a broad term identifying a fuller-bodied wine, sometimes with varying degrees of sweetness. Oloroso Sherries are much richer and darker than the two preceding types, and are fortified in the early stages to preserve their sweetness.

The sweeter commercial grades of Sherries are known as Creams. These are Olorosos that are given a back blend, or "dulce," or sweet unfermented must, either from the original lot or from lots made from Pedro Ximénez. Wines sold as Pedro Ximénez are selected sweet wines made exclusively from this noble grape; they have an intense sweetness, an unctuous texture and a rich raisiny flavor.

Finally, a few Sherry firms offer what are called Almacenistas. These are specific lots of wine produced by individual growers, selected and aged separately from a firms' regular production. They are considered reserve, hand-crafted lots of great individual character. They may cost a bit more than regular Sherry, but they are well worth it.

In order to maintain a consistent house style, all Sherry is produced from the time-honored solera system, whereby the casks of maturing wine are arranged in three tiers, each associated with the others in a continuous blending process, with the youngest wines on top and the oldest blends on the bottom. For this reason, few if any Sherries will carry a vintage date.

Major Producers:

Harvey's of Bristol, Gonzales, Byass (Tio Pepe), Williams & Humbert (Dry Sack), Sandeman, Pedro Domecq, Ferenando de Terry, Emilio Lustau, Wisdom & Warter, Osborne.

CYPRUS

Despite the close proximity of Cyprus to the Turkish mainland, the majority of the island population maintains strong Greek traditions, and there is a long heritage of quality winemaking. Many tourists in Cyprus soon become fond of the local wines, which are mostly grown in the center of the island around the Troodos Mountains.

Currently four main firms produce most of the wine for export: Keo, Sodap, Etko, and Loel. Their quality standards are for the most part high, and the wines can be found in most world markets. The table wines are popular, but arguably the island's best wine is Commandaria, a sweet dessert wine that traces its origins back to the twelfth Century, when it was prized by Knights Templar. Less alcoholic than Sherry, and less unctuous than most Marsalas, Commandaria keeps very well after opening and may be substituted for many other more expensive dessert wines.

Left: View of Kolossi castle, Cyprus, from the vineyards

Right: Watering of the vineyards is sometimes done in Greece due to its arid climate.

GREECE

Ancient Greece was the birthplace of wine in the ancient world. As is recorded in ancient legends and Homeric poems, wine was an important part of ancient Greek civilization, and it continues to this day.

Associated with Greece's recent entry in the European Common Market was an ambitious plan by the government to delimit some thirty new controlled appellations for Greek wine, taking into account traditional regions while recognizing those that have shown the most recent improvement. So far progress has been slow, but as the audience widens for better Greek wine, more will find its way into the international marketplace.

The oldest Greek wine tradition, which seems to be a practice unique to the country, is flavoring wine by mixing it with Aleppo pine resin – the source of the popular retsina. To many this odd, slightly medicinal beverage takes some getting used to, but it is a superb accom-

paniment to Greek food. It should be drunk young and fresh, and well-chilled to set off its piney flavor.

Another Greek specialty is Mavrodaphne, a sweet red wine that has now officially become an appellation. It is native to the Patras region near the Gulf of Corinth, and is produced by several firms. Many of the new Greek wine appellations hail from this area. Naossa, a powerful red wine from the region of Macedonia to the north, has recently been added to the list. Robola, a dry wine from Cephalonia near the Gulf of Corinth, has also achieved appellation status. Mavroudi, a red wine grown at Delphi and along the northern shore of the Gulf of Corinth, can be a fine accompaniment to food. Nemea, grown on the Peloponnesus, is another recent appellation noted for its reds. Potentially the reds of Metsovo, from the area near Epirus, are among the best of the group as they rely on Cabernet Sauvignon.

Much of the wine that is bottled and exported is sold by major wine shippers such as Achaia-Claus, Nicolaou and Cambas, which are based near the city of Patras but do not show an area of origin on their labels. Their brand names include "Demestica," "Pendeli" and "Santa Helena" which are all quite popular on the export market.

Left: Harvest time in Cephalonia, a Greek island near the Gulf of Corinth.

Right: Vineyards in the Vaud region of Switzerland, overlooking Lake Geneva. This is the home of Chasselas.

SWITZERLAND

Switzerland is a major wine-growing nation. The country's healthy wine consumption is partially offset by substantial imports from France and Italy, but in a few locations there is a proud tradition of wine-growing. The main problem with most Swiss wines is their high price – a function of high labor costs, limited production and the strong Swiss franc.

The Vaud and Valais areas are especially celebrated for their wines. The former lies on the north shore of Lake Geneva; the latter follows an extended valley to the east, sheltered by the towering Alps, and is one of the warmest and sunniest areas in Switzerland. Lake Geneva offers a fine environment for vineyards. The steep, terraced vineyards on its northern flank are well drained and well exposed to the sun, and the lake helps regulate the temperature.

Many Swiss growers rely on the Chasselas grape, a table grape noted for its mild, low acid wines that reflect its growing districts. Besides Chasselas, Switzerland has a wealth of other varieties, some of which are unique to the nation. Sylvaner, which is called Johannisberg in Switzerland, makes full, rounded wines that are excellent with food; Marsanne, the white grape of the northern Rhône, is called Ermitage and produces rich, exciting wines with plenty of body. Potentially

the biggest of the group is Malvoisie, the Swiss name for Pinot Gris or Pinot Grigio – like Italian Pinot Grigio, it has an enchanting pear flavor.

Swiss reds have much of the same style and charm. An example is Dole du Valais, a blend of Pinot Noir and Gamay; occasionally Petit Dole, made only from Gamay, is seen. Pinot Noir is usually called Blauburgunder in the German-speaking areas of Switzerland, or occasionally Klevner, and any wine sold as just Pinot Noir will be basic, sound and generally inexpensive.

Two other notable Swiss wine districts are Neuchatel, the area surrounding a lake of the same name, whose light, fresh Chasselas wines often have a faint sparkle relating to the practice of sur lie. Finally, in the Ticino district near the border with Italy, Merlot is grown for a fresh, attractive red wine called Merlot di Ticino.

Above: The vineyards of Aigle, one of the best Swiss winegrowing areas, on the eastern corner of Lake Geneva.

Left: The church of Riva San Vitale in the Ticino region of Switzerland, where an excellent Merlot is made.

Right: Vineyards in Steiermark (Styria), Austria.

Good Producers:

Bonvin, Hammel, Ville de Lausanne, Domaine du Mont d'Or, Orsat, Provins, Schenck, Testuz, Rouvinez.

AUSTRIA

Austria is one of eastern Europe's most important wine-growing nations. While no wine is grown in the mountainous western half of the country, the eastern half is home to many excellent wine regions. In Vienna, the nation's capital, there is an entire culture relating to the Heurigen, or wine taverns, that have been a part of Viennese life for over two hundred years.

Austrian wines are often compared with German wines, but in fact they are quite different. Not only are the informing grape varieties not the same, Austrian wines are usually somewhat drier in the same quality categories. This relates to the warmer, sunnier climate that prevails in most Austrian wine areas, as well as a national preference for enjoying wine with food.

In 1985 Austria revised a comprehensive wine law that set forth strict minimum quality grades. The law authorizes the following categories:

Qualitätswein (quality wine): The basic grades, which must have a minimum of 9% alcohol for white wines; 8.5% for reds. In practice, the wines are usually much more substantial and are usually rather good value.

Kabinett: Dry or semi dry wines produced from grapes with no sugar added. Legally, a better form of Qualitätswein, which may not exceed 12.7% alcohol.

Spätlese: Late harvested wines picked later in the season, slightly sweeter than Kabinett.

Auslese: Select late harvested wines, from grape bunches with unripe grapes removed. Usually quite sweet.

Beerenauslese: Very sweet wines produced from individually picked berries.

Ausbruch: An Austrian specialty: a super quality Beerenauslese made from overripe grapes, in a tradition dating back several centuries. Quite rare and intensely sweet.

Trockenbeerenauslese: Like the Spitzenweine of Germany; a rich, honeyed nectar made from dried, overripe grapes harvested late in the season. Very rare and very expensive.

Eiswein (Ice wine): Legally, a Beerenauslese made from grapes that must be frozen when harvested and pressed. Like German Eiswein, extremely sweet and very expensive; still essentially in a state of evolution. Many Ausbruchs are better.

As in Germany, white wines outnumber the reds in most Austrian wine districts. The national grape of Austria is the Grüner Veltliner, a fresh tasting vari-

ety grown all over the country and prized for its generous, quaffable wines; it should usually be drunk in its first year. Another good variety is Spätrot (also called Zierfandler), which is often blended together with Rotgipfler for added complexity. The German Riesling is called Rhein Riesling in Austria, to be distinguished from the lesser Welschriesling that is also grown. Müller-Thurgau is used for about 10% of all Austrian wines. Bouvier, an Austrian cross, makes exceptional late harvested wines in southern areas. Recently Weissburgunder, or Pinot Blanc, has become popular for its high quality dry white wines in the Burgundy style. Austrian reds tend to be soft and easygoing, but some have potential. One of the best is Blaufränkisch, or Gamay, which gives light fruity wines; on a limited basis the Pinot Noir, or Spätburgunder, gives superior results.

Vienna may be the biggest market, but Burgenland near Lake Neusiedl, a productive area that borders Hungary, is the biggest wine region with over 48,500 acres planted – divided into 3 separate districts. Neusiedl, named for the lake, is the biggest. The lake has an exceptionally warm, consistent climate, and some of the nation's best late harvested wines are grown here. Further north, in the Thermenregion (formerly Sudbahn) district, located just south of Vienna, the famous Gumpoldskirchner is grown, which is very popular in the capital. Kamptal, to the north, includes Austria's largest wine town, Langenlois, with a long quality record. A traditionally famous wine-growing area is the Danube Valley, which since 1985 has been delimited as Niederösterreich (lower Austria). Wachau, Donauland, Carnuntum and Steiermark (Styria) are supplementary districts. Growers: Lenz Moser in Burgenland is probably the largest and best known producer, but there are scores of others around the country: Josef Jamek in the Wachau, Wilhelm Bründelmayer in Langenois, Emmerich Knoll in Dürnstein, Franz Hirtzberger in Wachau, Martin Nigl in Kremstal, Josef Pöckl, Alois Kracher, Jost Höpler and Feiler-Artinger (the last four are all in Burgenland), are some of the more impressive new Austrian growers I have tasted recently.

Above: Vineyards in Burgenland, around harvest time.

Right: Vineyards in Lower Austria (Niederosterreich), when the leaves are just turning color.

HUNGARY

A national awareness of wine accompanies the rich, spicy Hungarian cuisine. With the collapse of communism in Eastern Europe in 1989, there is new excitement in Hungarian vineyards. Privatization has ironically restored many wine domaines to their original prewar status, and as the country continues its amazing economic boom, Hungary will once again be in the forefront of eastern European wine production.

Generally, with a few exceptions, Hungary's reds are superior to the whites, and they stand up well to the spicy, substantial paprikas and goulash that are part of Hungarian fare. The Hungarians have a long tradition of grape growing and wine production dating back to the Magyars.

Many Hungarian wines bear local names for grapes found in other countries. An example is Szürkebárat, meaning "gray friar," which is the same as Pinot Gris or Pinot Grigio; so called because of the shape of its leaves. Olaszrizling is the Hungarian name for Welsch Riesling. Leányka is an ancient white variety, found in Transylvania and in central Hungary and mostly grown for ordinary wine. Furmint is the grape essential to the legendary Tokay wine. The Kéknelyü grape gives the famous full white wines of Badacsony, while the Hárslevelü, or "lime leaf," is responsible for the notable wines of Debro in the Maatralya district. Recently some growers have turned away from these varieties and have planted Sauvignon Blanc and Chardonnay, with encouraging results.

Hungarian reds can be flavorful and substantial. Perhaps the best known is Egri Bikavér, or "bull's blood," native to the town of Eger. The most common red variety in Hungary is Kadarka and Kekfrankös which make light, quaffable reds similar to Beaujolais. Recently some growers have planted Cabernet Sauvignon with excellent results.

Hungary's largest production zone, the Alföld, in the center of the country, makes most of Hungary's ordinary wine. Some of Hungary's best wines come from Lake Balaton, the largest lake in Europe and overlooked by Badacsony, a massive volcanic hill with ideal vineyard soils, home of Badacsony Szürkebárat and Badacsony Kéknelyü. Besides Egri Bikavér and Villanyi Burgundi, there is a particularly good Cabernet wine grown near Hajos, sold as Hajosi Cabernet. The region of Szekszárd, in the south central zone, grows an especially fine Kadarka wine in the traditional style.

In the eastern extremes is the little village of Tokay, which produces Hungary's most famous white wine; noted especially for sweet wines that have been late harvested by selective picking.

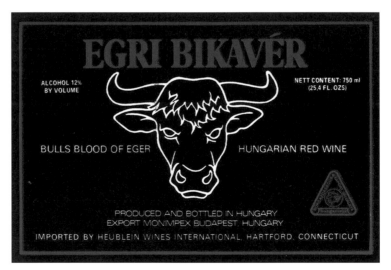

Right: Hungary's most famous white wine is Tokay, a delicious sweet wine that is late harvested.

The growers have established a classification to identify the grades of sweetness in Tokay: Szamarodni means "as it comes," the lightest and driest type of Tokay, made without any overripe grapes added. Aszú means "shriveled," grapes that have been late harvested and are richer in sugar. These are added to Szamarodni wines to build up the required sweetness. Puttonyos means "putt," a container of about 25 liters or 7 U.S. gallons which measures the Aszú grapes. The number of puttonyos added relates to the eventual sweetness; for Tokay Aszú, 3 puttonyos is the minimum and 6 puttonyos generally the sweetest commercial grade.

Eszenzia means "essence," a rare and extremely expensive form of Tokay, made only from the free-run juice exuded from grapes in the puttonyos waiting to be crushed. Because of the extraordinary high sugar content, this luscious wine ferments only to very low levels of alcohol and has amazing longevity.

Regardless of the level of sweetness, all Tokay has a family similarity: a light caramel hint in the background, resulting from a faint oxidation during the fermenting process, and a full, robust flavor. Its legendary powers that once resuscitated dying Russian Czars are definitely worth a try.

ROMANIA

Romania was called "Dacia" by the Romans, who were among the first to develop the vineyards in the third century B.C. Along with Hungary and Bulgaria, Romanian wine production was collectivized under communism, and the prewar system of small estates was abolished. But the collapse of communism in eastern Europe in 1989 threw Romania's wine industry in disarray, and the country was awash in a surplus of mediocre wine that nobody wanted. Almost all of the wine is being sold at very low prices, but since the quality varies considerably, it must be selected with care.

Among white grapes, the Chardonnay and Aligoté of Burgundy are common, but the former is apt to be vinified sweet. For red wines, Pinot Noir, Merlot and Cabernet Sauvignon are all grown in many areas, but they are usually much lighter and less distinctive than their French counterparts. A common grape in Romania is Feteasca, producing mild, easy-going white wines that are similar to the Leányka of Hungary. Many of the country's best sweet wines are made from Muskat Ottonel and Grasa.

Romania's Black Sea ports were early wine-growing centers. The mild, consistent climate was ideal for wine-growing, and two famous vineyards were founded: Cotnari, from the province of Moldavia; and Murfatlar to the south, developed some years later, which produces similar sweet wines. During the 1950s the state dramatically expanded vineyards in several inland areas: Focşani, the Tirnave district in Transylvania, and a major new vineyard at Dealul Mare along the

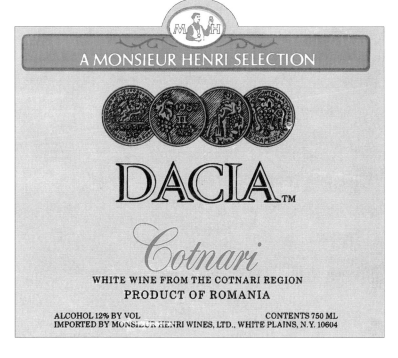

Below: The Romanian wine industry is experiencing a lot of changes with the fall of Communism, as smaller estates are starting to come into their own.

Carpathian Mountains. Many of the best grape varieties are grown in these newer wine producing areas.

The two main labels for export by the Romanian State Monopoly are Premiat, a label used by Pepsico in the U.S., and Mehana, which is seen in Great Britain. In addition, smaller estates are now beginning to enter the market and sell under their own labels.

BULGARIA

Bulgaria has a long tradition of high quality wines and shares many of the same viticultural advantages as Romania, with a slightly longer growing season resulting from her southerly exposure. The state monopoly Vinprom is a major producer, directing over 150 cooperative cellars. A new law of controlled appellation, Controli-ran, was introduced in 1985 to promote higher quality wine for export. "Reserve" wines, which enjoy some wood and bottle age, are also becoming popular.

Bulgaria grows almost all of the major French varieties, with a few indigenous grapes of her own. Among white grapes, Chardonnay and Sauvignon Blanc are commonly seen, and the former is increasingly aged in oak for improved flavor. For red wines, Pinot Noir, Merlot and Cabernet Sauvignon are grown in many areas, but are usually lighter and less distinctive than their French counterparts. A common grape in Bulgaria is Dimiat, producing mild, easy-going white wines. Many of the country's best sweet wines are made from Fetiaska, Misket (Muscat) and Grasa.

The largest white wine district in Bulgaria is the Shumen area in the eastern part of the country. Suhindol in the north is another traditional wine name, the site of the country's first cooperative (1909) and lately the focus of modernization and expansion. The Bulgarian Controliran grows mostly reds and includes Lozitza, a northern region prized for its Cabernet Sauvignon. Much of Bulgaria's Chardonnay comes from well-suited vineyards in Varna, near the Black Sea

A MONSIEUR HENRI SELECTION

ALCOHOL 12%
BY VOLUME

NET CONTENTS
750ML

TRAKIA™
1983

CHARDONNAY
DRY WHITE WINE FROM THE SHUMEN REGION
APPELLATION OF ORIGIN

PRODUCED AND BOTTLED IN BULGARIA BY VINIMPEX, SOFIA
IMPORTED BY MONSIEUR HENRI WINES, LTD., WHITE PLAINS, N.Y. 10604

Below: Bulgaria has a long tradition of making good quality wines at fair prices.

coast. Newer vineyards which are just developing nearby at Novi Pazar are potentially even finer.

The two main labels for export by the Bulgarian State Monopoly are Trakia, a label used by Pepsico in the U.S.; and Iskra, used for sparkling wine. In addition, as in Romania, independent estates are now entering the market with their own labels.

ISRAEL

Palestine is an ancient vineyard, where traditions are strong but not strong enough to stand in the way of many winemaking innovations. Grape growing in Israel today is a modern science. To grow grapes in the parched desert, Israeli scientists developed the drip-flow system of irrigation that is now standard practice in many arid wine regions. There are now over 20,000 acres of vineyards.

Israel is a major supplier to the important kosher market worldwide. To be called kosher, a wine must be produced under strict rabbinical supervision by observant Jews. Only approved winemaking additives may be used in winemaking, and no animal-based products are allowed. If a kosher wine is also "mevushal," it has gone through a heating process similar to pasteurization. Formerly this degraded the wine, but for today's mevushal wines the juice is usually heated before winemaking begins, thus minimizing its effect on flavor.

Sauvignon Blanc and Chardonnay are currently the most successful white varieties, especially the latter, if given appropriate aging in oak prior to bottling. Cabernet Sauvignon and Merlot distinguish the red wine offerings, especially if blended together in the Bordeaux style. Emerald Riesling, Sémillon, Chenin Blanc and Muscat are still important for the traditional market, as are ports and other fortified wines.

In the 1880s Baron Edmond de Rothschild began a major expansion of vineyards in the country that provided the basis for today's production. The largest wine region in the country is Richon-le-Zion south of Tel Aviv, followed by Zichron-Jacob to the north. A productive region is the Samson district in the

southeastern corner, where many of the nation's biggest wineries produce in volume. The Carmel Wine Company is a well-known producer.

One of the newest wine areas in Israel is the Golan Heights, near the border with Syria, where the Golan Heights Winery was founded in 1983. The special location near high Mount Hermon is well-suited to premium grape varieties. The winery sells under three different labels: Gamla, Golan, and Yarden, the latter being reserved for the best lots.

Opposite: Carmel Wines aging in oak and redwood cooperage.

Left: Freshly harvested grapes arrive at the modern facilities of the Carmel Wine Company.

Below: Mechanical harvesting machines are used at the Carmel vineyards.

THE NEW WORLD

THE UNITED STATES

There is a lot more cheer among American winegrowers now than there was seven years ago. When major political issues relating to the role of alcohol in society were hurting wine sales: drunk-driving fatalities were a national concern and warning labels began to appear on wine bottles sold in the United States.

But in view of recent medical statistics, which suggest that wine consumption may have health benefits, the picture has changed. The "French Paradox" television program in 1991, highlighted the value of wine in French diets, and now there is the "Mediterranean Diet," based on grains, vegetables, olive oil and wine.

CALIFORNIA

With its sunny location and a regular, consistent climate, much of California is perfect for vineyards. Vines were first planted in the state in 1769 by Franciscan missionaries, but California's wine-making heritage is only about a century old, and its real impact on national and international wine markets is only decades old.

There are several geographic factors that make California's vineyards special. The first is their location, east of a series of coastal mountain ranges that block rainfall and winds moving in from the Pacific Ocean. Another is a highly predictable rainfall pattern, whereby the wine regions are very dry for most of the year, allowing a steady and dependable growing season. The climate in most areas is warm and mild, with little danger of spring frost.

The notion of specific sites for vineyards has come late to California. In the past, land was set aside for vines based on what was available, not what had been judged optimum for grapes. During the past decade, California's growers have paid increasing attention to selected vineyard sites, optimizing the best grape varieties and adapting the right growing techniques. The concept of viticultural areas, now officially sanctioned by the U.S. government, means that grape sources can be precisely identified. In 1861 Count Agoston Haraszthy, known as "the father of California viticulture," was commissioned by state governor John Downey to bring back vine cuttings from Europe and thereby establish California as a major wine-growing area.

Previous pages: Acres of vineyards in the Sonoma Valley, California.

Left: Old California vines in the spring, when the wild mustard blooms.

Above: The Napa County line, as seen from the air.

Right: Beautiful plantings at the Stag's Leap Cellars in the Stag's Leap district of the Napa Valley.

✿ Napa ✿

The Napa Valley begins some thirty miles northeast of San Francisco, in the headwaters of San Pablo Bay, and in its southern extremities lies the flat area known as the Carneros, shared with Sonoma County to the west. Westward, the Mayacamas Mountain range forms a protective barrier to the sea; eastward, another set of mountain ranges contains air flow over the valley and permits a daily cycling of warm daytime and cool nighttime air, beneficial to the vines.

The central Napa Valley, beginning at Yountville and extending north for about 20 miles, is the traditional focal point for the California wine industry. This area includes the Rutherford Bench (ideal for Cabernet Sauvignon), the Stag's Leap growing district, and the Mount Veeder appellation on the western hills overlooking the valley floor. The northern Napa Valley is warmer than the southern section, and many vineyards on the valley floor are especially fertile. Those situated on steep hillside vineyards produce considerably less than those on the valley floor, but either location can make outstanding wine in the right vintages. Proceeding from St. Helena to Angwin and Calistoga, the climate gets progressively hotter and is not always suitable to certain white grape varieties. But in upland areas, particularly in Howell Mountain and Pope Valley, the climate stays cool

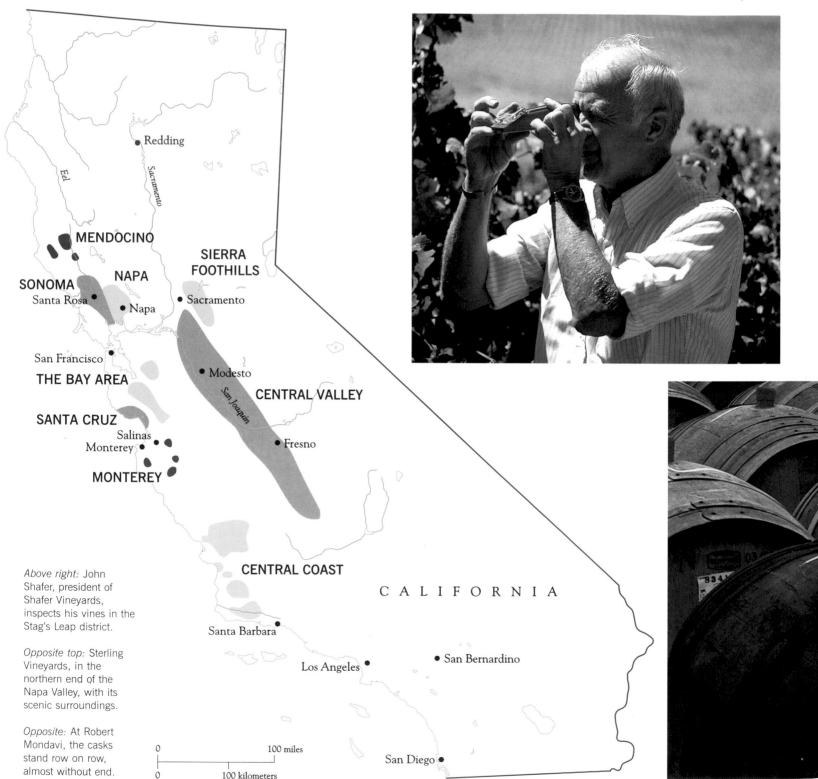

Above right: John Shafer, president of Shafer Vineyards, inspects his vines in the Stag's Leap district.

Opposite top: Sterling Vineyards, in the northern end of the Napa Valley, with its scenic surroundings.

Opposite: At Robert Mondavi, the casks stand row on row, almost without end.

and the soil and exposure is especially good. At Calistoga the Napa Valley reaches its northernmost extremity.

The Napa Valley is particularly noted for Cabernet Sauvignon, a variety that was brought to the Valley over a century ago and quickly established its reputation. In recent years, some wineries have supplanted Cabernet Sauvignon with the other four Bordeaux varieties: Cabernet Franc, Merlot, Malbec and Petit-Verdot, either on their own or in blends. These varieties may be combined, as in Bordeaux, for a "Meritage" type of wine. [There are also some white Meritage wines, crafted from Sauvignon Blanc and Sémillon.]

Zinfandel, California's unique contri-

bution to the wine world, has found some ideal niches in the Napa Valley especially in some mountain vineyards where its spicy fruit flavor can find full expression. Petite Sirah (or Duriff) is another colorful red grape; Napa Valley Petite Sirahs can produce some memorable bottles. A few Napa Valley growers have even grown the true Syrah grape of France's Rhône Valley, and have had excellent results.

Among white varieties, Chardonnay reigns supreme in the Napa Valley, where its lush, opulent styles recall some of the best white Burgundy. Chardonnay generally does best in cooler hillside vineyards that are well-drained. It also excels in French oak barrels, which give the right flavor and complexity. But Chardonnay is not the only outstanding white grape in the Napa Valley. Many leading wineries prefer Sauvignon Blanc (sometimes sold as Fumé Blanc, if made from 100% varietal and given some barrel aging), because it can produce a wide variety of styles and expressions in dry white wines. Chenin Blanc, while less popular than it once was, still makes an attractive sipping wine.

Vineyards in the Napa Valley officially begin in the Carneros district to the south. Only recently has the area been planted in wine grapes, but a few

Left: Domaine Chandon, in the Napa Valley, makes extensive use of stainless steel tanks in the production of sparkling wine.

Below: Early morning fog in the Napa Valley, part of the unique microclimate that makes the valley ideal for grape growing.

Right: The grand entrance hall at Opus One, a premium winery in the Napa Valley.

pioneers led the way. Acacia, Saintsbury and Robert Sinskey Vineyards have been celebrated for their excellent Chardonnays and Pinot Noirs. Bouchaine Vineyards, Kent Rasmussen and Carneros Creek complete the roster of the producers in the Carneros district.

Further north, a new generation has taken over at Charles Krug, where the Peter Mondavi family is continuing over a century's worth of winemaking fame. Further down the road, the Robert Mondavi Winery stands testament to an unprecedented family success story. Their wines rank with some of the country's best and are consistent best sellers. Likewise, a younger generation now heads the Louis M. Martini Winery, which for decades has produced benchmark Cabernet Sauvignon. In Rutherford, Beaulieu Vineyard's venerable Beautour, Rutherford and Private Reserve Cabernet Sauvignons are still much in demand. Franciscan Vineyards is now making some of their best wines ever.

Newer wineries have added to Napa's fame in recent years. Dunn Vineyards produces superb Cabernets from Howell

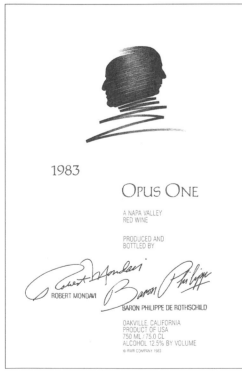

1983

OPUS ONE

A NAPA VALLEY
RED WINE

PRODUCED AND
BOTTLED BY

ROBERT MONDAVI

BARON PHILIPPE DE ROTHSCHILD

OAKVILLE, CALIFORNIA
PRODUCT OF USA
750 ML / 75.0 CL
ALCOHOL 12.5% BY VOLUME
© RMR COMPANY 1983

Mountain, and advises Pahlmeyer Vineyards. Von Strasser Winery is one of the newest and most promising of these super premium Cabernet growers.

Sterling Vineyards in Calistoga opened in 1972 and various corporate takeovers obliged Peter Newton, one of its original investors, to establish his own winery, Newton Vineyards, in 1978. The Hess Collection Winery is now both a winemaking and artistic showcase. Atlas Peak Vineyard, an international project begun by Whitbread-Antinori in the late 1980s, is now producing Italian styled varietals on Atlas Peak in the southeastern corner of the valley. Beringer Vineyards, a venerable producer of Napa Valley wines for over a century, is now making some outstanding new wines. Clos du Val, begun by Frenchman Bernard Portet in 1970, makes a unique statement about Stag's Leap District Cabernet Sauvignon; his neighbors, Stag's Leap Vineyard and Stag's Leap Wine Cellars have continued success with Cabernet. Another successful Stag's Leap District operation is Shafer Vineyards, founded in 1972 and now making exquisite Cabernets and Merlots. Chimney Rock is another noted Stag's Leap producer; Steltzner Vineyards was famous as a grape grower long before they established winemaking facilities of their own. Pine Ridge Winery sells some of their best wines under that appellation – and Silverado Vineyards completes this impressive roster of producers in the Stag's Leap District.

Sparkling wine used to constitute only a small proportion of Napa Valley wines. The only players were Hanns Kornell, who recently ceased operations, and Schramsberg Winery, which makes brilliant but relatively rare sparkling wines. This all changed in 1973, when the French conglomerate Moët & Hennessy established their Napa winery, called Domaine Chandon, to produce high quality sparkling wine via the Champagne method. They now have rivals in Domaine Carneros, an impressive operation owned by Champagne Taittinger; Domaine Mumm, under the direction of Mumm's of Champagne; and Codorniu Napa, owned and operated by the Spanish firm Codorniu.

For years, Napa boasted dozens of small wineries whose limited production and high quality put them in high demand. Today, many of these wineries are still small and exclusive. A prime example is Mayacamas Vineyards, over a century old but owned for over two decades by Robert Travers. Mount Veeder Winery, Smith-Madrone and

Ritchie Creek Wineries next door contributed much to the early fame of the Mount Veeder appellation with a series of outstanding Cabernets. Stony Hill Winery, begun over fifty years ago by the late Fred McCrea, is still making first-rate Chardonnays. Veteran winemaker Joseph Heitz has handed the baton for his Heitz Cellars to his children, and they continue in the same fine tradition. Next door, Joseph Phelps Winery has expanded their operation, and their super-premium Meritage wine, "Insignia," ranks as one of California's best. The same could be said for noted Bordeaux winemaker Christian Moueix, whose "Dominus" aspires to the same heights as his Pomerols and Saint-Emilions. Famous Hollywood director Francis Ford Coppola fashions an equally prized and popular Meritage blend called "Rubicon" from his Niebaum-Coppola Estate Winery.

Meritage wines are hardly limited to these producers. One of the most famous Franco-American alliances took place in 1979 when Robert Mondavi decided to link up with the late Baron Philippe de Rothschild, proprietor of Château Mouton-Rothschild in Bordeaux, and created a Bordeaux-styled blend called Opus One. Opus One made its debut in 1984, and has been fetching accolades ever since. Flora Springs Winery also makes a super premium Meritage wine in a rather fuller style, called Trilogy. Duckhorn Vineyards is famous for their outstanding Merlots and Cabernet Sauvignons.

Making great Cabernet is one of the Napa Valley's traditions. It came easily to Charles Wagner, Sr., who founded Caymus Vineyards in 1972; his son Chuck is at least as gifted a winemaker. Cuvaison Winery grew famous very early for Cabernet Sauvignon and has maintained its reputation. Raymond Vineyard recently expanded and the wines are now finer than ever. Far Niente Winery and Freemark Abbey turn out some super-premium Cabernets and Chardonnays year after year. Miljenko ("Mike") Grgich founded Grgich Cellars in 1976; now his sleek, crafted wines are much in demand. Grgich has some distinguished company in the vicinity: Sequoia Grove, noted for their Cabernets and Chardonnays; Cakebread, an established Napa label, now making a whole new improved series of

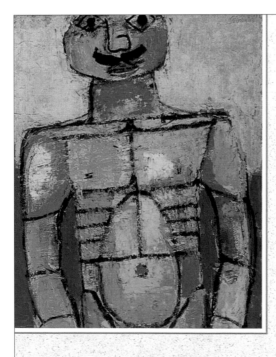

*Jean Dubuffet
(1901-1988)
Nu Chamarre
1943*

HOMMAGE
1988
Red Table Wine
California

PRODUCED AND
BOTTLED BY
CLOS PEGASE,
CALISTOGA, CA

CLOS PEGASE

Above left: A luncheon table is set at Sequoia Grove, in the Napa Valley.

Left: The spectacular mountain vineyards of Cain Vineyards and Cellars, Napa.

Above: The tasting room at Sebastiani Cellars, Sonoma.

wines; Turnbull (formerly Johnson-Turnbull) Wine Cellars, famous for their elegant Cabernets; De Moor, owned by a Belgian company, with finely crafted Cabernets and Chardonnays; Groth, a first-rate producer of Cabernet; Girard, equally skilled with Chardonnay and Cabernet; Silver Oak, an ultra-premium winery specializing only in Cabernet, and Cosentino Winery.

Robert Keenan has produced good Chardonnays and Cabernets for almost twenty years. Cain Cellars makes an extremely fine Meritage red called "Cain Five," identifying all five Bordeaux varietals. Tom Burgess took over Lee Stewart's original Souverain Winery and renamed it Burgess Cellars. Long Vineyards is famous for their rare, exquisite Chardonnays.

Trefethen, near St. Helena, makes a wide assortment of good wines; the Corley family can be proud of the many excellent wines produced at Monticello Winery. Conn Creek is noted for their sturdy Cabernets; Villa Mount Eden, with equally good Chardonnay; Spring Mountain and St. Clement and Rutherford Hill Winery make excellent varietals; and Spottswoode is a small winery dedicated to rich Cabernet Sauvignons. Frogs Leap Winery's catchy name and label sometimes overshadow the good wines they make; Rombauer Vineyards, another top producer, identifies their best wine "le meilleur du chai."

Other notable Napa Valley wineries

Left: Riddling racks at Gloria Ferrer sparkling wine cellars, Sonoma.

Below: Aerial photo of Glen Ellen Winery, Sonoma.

Right: Marimar Torres, of the famous Spanish winemaking family, now has her own cellars in Sonoma and makes excellent wine.

include: Markham, Costello, Lakespring, William Hill, Merryvale Vintners, Peju Province, Quail Ridge, Robert Pepi (now owned by Kendall-Jackson), Z.D. Cellars, Sullivan, Clos Pegase (a noted architectural showplace), Tudal, Tulocay, Whitehall Lane, Folie à Deux, Château Potelle (owned by a French winemaking couple), and Vichon, now managed by Robert Mondavi. On a much grander scale is Sutter Home Winery, which graced many an American table with their White Zinfandels in the 1980s, sometimes overshadowing their other good varietals.

Not all Napa growers specialize in Cabernet Sauvignon. A few, like Storybook Mountain Vineyards in Calistoga, specialize in Zinfandel, as does Lamborn Family Vineyards on Howell Mountain. In the northern extremes of the Valley, Robert Pecota Winery is especially noted for their fragrant white wines, and Château Montelena Winery for their benchmark Cabernet Sauvignons – after all, it was Château Montelena, and Stag's Leap Wine Cellars, who in 1976 proved to an all-French jury in Paris that California wines could sometimes outclass some of France's most famous producers.

❧ Sonoma ❧

Sonoma actually has more acres of vineyard than Napa, but because they are more spread out in different districts, Sonoma's wineries do not share the same sort of recognition. The first wineries were initially constructed around the Sonoma Mission itself. Sonoma's climatic diversity is greater than Napa's. The county's lower reaches include the Carneros district, where conditions are consistently cool. Then the climate gets warmer in Sonoma Valley to the north, a viticultural district protected by tall mountain barriers, only to turn cool once again in the Russian River Valley, from the proximity to the Pacific Ocean. Following the Russian River's course upstream from Guerneville, the climate gets progressively warmer in the Alexander Valley. Most of the biggest and best-known Sonoma wineries lie in the Alexander Valley, where they profit from the productive soil and ideal growing conditions.

The first bonded winery in Sonoma was Buena Vista, which dates back to 1857. Today, under the direction of the Moller-Racké family, the wines are better than ever. Gundlach-Bundschu Winery was started over a century ago by German immigrants, and their superb Merlots have won many awards. The Rodney Strong label identifies sound wines in the moderate price ranges.

A germinal figure in Sonoma winegrowing was the late James D. Zellerbach, former ambassador to France, who established Hanzell Winery in 1956 and determined that oak imported from

France was the missing ingredient to crafting great Chardonnay – the die was cast for the future of California winemaking. Nearby, Haywood Winery produces sound, popularly priced varietals. Carmenet Winery is an ultra-premium operation and many of their recent vintages have been superb.

Sebastiani is another major force in Sonoma. Besides their main label, their volume label Vendange has become very popular. Samuel Sebastiani, who helped contribute to much of the company's rapid growth in the 1980s, has now established his own operation known as Viansa, in the Carneros district. A neighbor specializing in sparkling wines is Gloria Ferrer, controlled by the Ferrer family that directs Freixenet, a sparkling wine producer in Catalonia, Spain. Ravenswood, to the north, is a celebrated producer of Zinfandels.

Many early wineries were founded in the Sonoma Valley, because of its excellent soils and climate. Today, one of the most visible wineries in the area is Glen Ellen, founded by the Benziger family of New York: after many years of successfully building Glen Ellen, the Benzigers sold it so they could concentrate on their premium label, Benziger. Elsewhere in the valley, Saint Francis Winery makes a particularly fine Merlot and Kunde Vineyards excels at Chardonnay. Laurel Glen,

Grand Cru Winery, H. Coturri, B.R. Cohn and Valley of the Moon are other notable wine producers in this historic growing area.

One of the most dramatic wineries in Sonoma Valley is Château St. Jean. Although former winemaker Dick Arrowood left in 1986 to form the celebrated Arrowood Vineyards, Château St. Jean is still one of the state's top producers – especially with vineyard designated wines. Kistler Winery's Chardonnays and Pinot Noirs rank with California's best. Up Bennett Valley Road is Matanzas Creek Winery, who craft superb Chardonnays, Sauvignon Blancs and stunning Merlots. On the other side of a dividing ridge of mountains is La Crema Winery, which makes good Pinot Noirs.

Named for Russian settlers who first came to the area in the 18th century, the Russian River district includes many outstanding wineries. The largest producer in the area is F. Korbel & Bros. in Guerneville, which has been making some of America's finest méthode champenoise sparkling wines for a century. Piper-Sonoma, owned by Piper-Heidsieck came to the county in 1980 and soon established a fine reputation.

One of California's most successful wineries is Kendall-Jackson, originally from Lake County but now headquartered in Santa Rosa and making elegant, moderately priced wines in volume. Elsewhere in the Russian River, De Loach Vineyards crafts a variety of excellent wines under the Russian River appellation. Sonoma-Cutrer Vineyards, an enterprise started by Bryce Cutrer Jones in 1981, makes only high-end Chardonnays from three different sources in Sonoma County. Two other noted producers in the area are Adler Fels and Fisher Vineyards.

Many new vintners have chosen the Russian River Valley because of its superior climate and soils. Williams-Selyem Winery makes some superb Pinot Noirs; Hanna Winery makes excellent Cabernets and Chardonnays. Z. Moore crafts an outstanding Gewürztraminer; Marimar Torres, from the famous house of Torres in Spain, now has her own superb winery near Sebastopol. Iron Horse is world-famous for its elegant sparkling wines made by the méthode champenoise. Taft Street Winery, Davis Bynum and Belvedere are all noted producers of popularly priced varietals. Across the valley, in the Chalk Hill area, Chalk Hill Winery has a new series of fine, moderately priced wines. Sotoyome, J. Rochioli and Rabbit Ridge round out the list of impressive Chalk Hill producers.

Because the Alexander Valley is so conducive to large-scale wine-growing, many of the biggest Sonoma County wineries have their operations there. A prime example is Geyser Peak, which recently hired Australian winemaker Darryl Groom to totally transform it.

Left: Davis Bynum, a veteran of the California wine industry, in his Sonoma cellars.

Above right: Dry Creek, a famous Sonoma producer, is synonymous with good Zinfandel.

Below right: Hop kilns were once common throughout northern California. This one now identifies an excellent grower of Zinfandel.

property of Ridge Vineyards, is celebrated for their rich, intense Zinfandels.

Simi Winery grew to be a world-class operation under famous winemaker Zelma Long. Their Cabernets and Chardonnays have been memorable. White Oak Vineyards makes some excellent Chardonnays and Cabernets; Hop Kiln makes some extraordinary Zinfandels. Louis Foppiano's family has been growing wines in the area for over a century; the Seghesio family originated as a bulk red wine producer but now is an excellent grower of moderately priced premium wines.

The Dry Creek area to the west has notably different soils and climate. David Stare of Boston helped popularize the name Dry Creek, and many of his wines grew famous. A. Rafanelli Winery has been a particularly noted producer of Zinfandel; Quivira Winery limits their efforts to Zinfandel and Sauvignon Blanc. Robert Stemmler and Domaine Michel are also well established. Preston Vineyards continually makes some of the best Zinfandels and Sauvignon Blancs in the area. Ferrari-Carano Winery, founded in 1981, has produced some extraordinary wines at their new, state-of-the-art facilities. Bandiera Winery is the most northerly winery in Sonoma before Mendocino County begins. Their elegant labels suggest the sleek, affordable wines they make.

Similarly, Clos du Bois Winery makes unique statements about northern Sonoma with their "Calcaire" and "Flintwood" Chardonnays, "Briarcrest" Cabernet Sauvignon, and "Marlstone" Meritage wines. Jordan Winery, originally specialized only in Cabernet Sauvignon and Chardonnay and recently added an outstanding sparkling wine, called "J."

The Wetzel family founded Alexander Valley Vineyards in 1962, and have contributed a great deal to the area's heritage. Their neighbors Johnson's Alexander Valley Winery and Field Stone sprang up soon afterwards and soon acquired a fine reputation. Next door, Château Souverain Winery is now turning out some very fine wines. Trentadue ("32," in Italian) makes some good Zinfandels. DeLorimer Winery has done well in recent judgings. Lytton Springs, now the

Left: Fetzer, the driving force in Mendocino County.

Below: A typical California bottling line.

Right: Vineyards managed by Wente Bros., the original vintners in Alameda County.

❧ Mendocino ❧

Mendocino is the coolest and most northerly of the three principal North Coast counties. A rugged, mountainous region, Mendocino grows especially refined and scented white wines, some exceptional sparkling wines, and a few good reds in well exposed vineyards. Chardonnay and Sauvignon Blanc do exceptionally well in Mendocino's cool climate. A few growers realize Riesling's inherent potential, which is usually masked in warmer climates further south; the same applies to Gewürztraminer, which gives excellent results here. Zinfandel dominates the red grape varieties; many wineries have repeatedly demonstrated how much at home it is here. The cool climate brings out the true fruit and fragrance of Pinot Noir as well. Cabernet Sauvignon is less of a factor here than it is further south, although some growers plant it with Merlot and its relative, Cabernet Franc, to make a refined and delicious Meritage wine.

The primary force in the county today is Fetzer, which recently celebrated its 25th year of wine-growing. Although Fetzer is no longer family-owned, it has become a major factor on the market and the wines are usually excellent. The big Dunnewood operation nearby, now owned by Guild, gives Fetzer some serious competition in the lower price ranges. Weibel Cellars recently moved from Fremont to new facilities in the county: their wines are steadily improving. A new producer located some distance away, Wildhurst Vinyards, completes this roster of wineries who aim to provide wines in the all-important midrange price category.

Another venerable producer is Parducci Cellars, who spearheaded the Mendocino County appellation. Konocti Winery in Lakeport is another large operation; they make a wide range of good wines, including a Meritage series. The famous nineteenth century actress Lily Langtree is closely identified with Guenoc Winery and their elegant, flavorful wines are consistently good, while their Meritage series are exceptional. McDowell Valley Vineyards in Hopland have an interesting range of varietals from the Rhône.

Sparkling wines are another specialty of the county. Scharffenberger has grown to a respectable midsize winery with national distribution. Nearby, Roederer Estate is one of the county's finer sparkling wines.

Some Mendocino wineries have been reincarnated; a recent example is Edmeades Winery, with many excellent vintages to their credit. Hidden Cellars in Ukiah has produced some remarkable wines under winemaker Greg Graziano; Graziano also has a small operation of his own called "Domaine St. Gregory" that has produced some interesting Italian-style varietals. Navarro Vineyards in Philo crafts some medal winning Chardonnays and Rieslings; Milano Winery in Hopland has a broad array of reds.

Gabrielli Cellars is barely five years old, but is already making some terrific Zinfandel; Frey Vineyards has an especially broad range of wines. Jepson Vineyards nearby has crafted some good white wine, some superb sparkling wine, and even a little brandy. And, when it comes to California brandy, try Germain-Robin – crafted by a Frenchman, Hubert Germain-Robin.

✤ The Bay Area ✤

The San Francisco Bay area is one of California's traditional wine regions. Its large population and superb transportation facilities established it very early as a prime market for the developing wine industry. The eastern section of the bay is planted extensively in Sauvignon Blanc and Chardonnay. Because of differences in the climate and soils, red wines have been less successful, with the possible exception of some Cabernet Sauvignons and Zinfandels.

Two winemaking families, the Wentes and the Concannons, are traditionally famous in this area. The Wente Bros. Winery has been under continuous family ownership since they were established in 1883, and in addition to a full line of table wines, they founded a sparkling wine facility in 1980 that has been a huge success. Concannon Vineyard dates back to the same time; they have always been noted for good Petite Sirah, and their legendary Sauvignon Blanc.

Ivan Tamás Winery, also in Livermore, is a new arrival with some good Cabernet Sauvignons and Chardonnays to their credit; Fenestra Cellars grows varietals traditional to the area and does a creditable job. Elsewhere, Rosenblum Cellars in Alameda has a great collection of different Zinfandels.

South of San Francisco Bay, the Santa Clara district has an important cluster of vineyards. This family-owned winery has become a major player in the area, and their wines are now better than ever. J. Lohr Winery, managed by the energetic Jerry Lohr, also draws from grapes grown in Monterey. Mount Eden Vineyards in Saratoga produces small quantities of exquisite but pricy Cabernet, Pinot Noir and Chardonnay.

Established in 1959, Ridge Vineyards in Cupertino is often called "the house of Zinfandel" because of their continued success with that varietal. Kathryn Kennedy Winery in Saratoga has a fabulous local reputation; Woodside Vineyards in Woodside was one of the first in the area. Thomas Fogarty Winery in Woodside makes a particularly elegant Chardonnay; Sunrise Winery, Page Mill Winery and Jory Winery also produce notable wines.

✤ Santa Cruz ✤

The hilly, remote pine forests of Santa Cruz County are a totally different world from many of the other California wine districts. While the total acreage may be small (less than 140 acres), the wines reflect a craftsmanship and originality that is rare in some of the bigger California wine districts. The hilly terrain is the limiting factor in Santa Cruz. Most varieties are very successful; in particular, Pinot Noir and Riesling grow especially well here, profiting from the cool climate. But Chardonnay continues to be the most popular variety.

Hallcrest Vineyards was one of the first wineries to squarely put Santa Cruz on the map and now specializes in organic wines. San Jose dermatologist David Bruce established his winery in 1964 and soon became famous for very individual, often spectacular wines. Roudon-Smith is a traditional Cabernet producer; Ken Burnap of Santa Cruz Mountain Vineyard is an excellent maker of rich, textured Pinot Noirs.

An eccentric but brilliant winemaker is Randall Grahm of Bonny Doon Vineyards, one of the original "Rhône Rangers" who successfully pioneered Rhône and Italian varietals in California. Ahlgren Vineyard makes a delicious Cabernet Franc; Storrs Winery produces an excellent Chardonnay.

❧ Monterey ❧

Monterey is a relatively new California wine district, although its agricultural potential was known long before producers began planting vineyards here in the 1960s. Now that most of the vineyards are mature, it is clear that Monterey is an exceptional wine-growing region. The Pacific Ocean plays an important role in many California wine districts, but here its effect is even more significant. Differences between cool water temperatures and the warm landmass bring in daily fog, which keeps the vineyards cool for much of the growing season; November harvests are not uncommon in the Monterey region, giving the grapes a lot of time to develop better acid balance and more flavor. The primary vineyards begin near

Above: The entrance to Chalone Vineyards, one of the top growers in Monterey County.

Left: Vineyards in the Greenfield area of Monterey County, nestled along the Coast Range.

Above right: Harvest at Bonny Doon Vineyards, in the Central Coast. Bonny Doon is known for their innovative wines.

the town of Salinas, and extend southwards on either side of Highway 101 over a 40 mile (64 km) stretch.

The area as a whole is quite propitious to Chardonnay, and in some vineyards Riesling has produced phenomenal results. Pinot Noir is very much at home in the cool climate and chalky soil. The quality of some late harvested wines is far superior to many wines from other North Coast counties.

A prime example of Monterey's recent growth is the Monterey Vineyard, specializing in moderately priced wines with the Monterey appellation. Another major operation is Jekel Vineyard whose Chardonnays, Merlots and Cabernets are excellent. Morgan Winery near Salinas specializes in Chardonnay and Pinot Noir. Tucked away in the hills near Soledad is another famous winery, Chalone, who makes probably the best Pinot Blanc in the state, along with Chardonnay. Another outstanding Chardonnay producer in the area is Robert Talbott Vineyards in Gonzales.

Bernardus Winery makes a scented Pinot Noir; Doug Meador's Ventana Winery produces particularly fine Chardonnays, and Château Julien has a wide range of popularly-priced wines. Monterey Peninsula Winery has long been famous for their rich, intense Zinfandels.

Sadly, in nearby San Benito, famous Almaden Vineyards has essentially turned into a jug wine producer. Nearby, Josh Jensen's Calera Wine Co. ("lime," in Spanish) was founded over a lime outcropping, and they now make some spectacular Pinot Noirs from designated single vineyards.

✿ Central Coast ✿

The term "central coast" includes several coastal counties in close proximity, located about midway between the cities of San Francisco and Los Angeles. In general, the climate in the central coast area is much like that in Monterey – subject to the same cooling influence from the chilly Pacific Ocean.

There are four distinct segments of the Central Coast. In the north, around the city of Paso Robles, there is a cluster of wineries and vineyards well known to lovers of Zinfandel. Then, about 24 miles (40 km) to the south, near the city of San Luis Obispo, the Edna Valley district includes some major wineries, many of them fairly new. Further south, near the city of Los Alamos, lies the bountiful Santa Maria Valley, an area that furnishes grapes for many wineries in the state. Finally, in Santa Barbara County, lie the vineyards of the fertile Santa Ynez Valley and the areas around Santa Barbara itself.

The central coast is best suited for cool climate grapes. It is already clear that Pinot Noir and Chardonnay excel in many districts, particularly in Santa Maria and Santa Barbara. Another variety that stands out in the Paso Robles district is Zinfandel, which has elegant fruit and finesse. Many of the area's wineries have successfully experimented with the grape varieties native to the

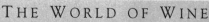

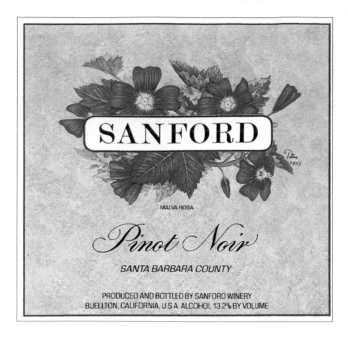

Below: Vineyards belonging to the Edna Valley Winery in the San Luis Obispo area.

Far right: The York Mountain Winery in the Paso Robles area makes exceptional Zinfandel.

Rhône district in France, reflecting a new popular demand for wines of this type. Syrah especially excels in the central coast, where it gives smooth, deeply colored wines with a spicy flavor.

A number of producers in the Paso Robles area excel with Zinfandel. York Mountain Winery in Templeton was one of the first; Adelaida Cellars and Mastan-tuono are other good producers in the area. Martin Brothers was an original pioneer in red Italian varietals; most notably, their Nebbiolos have stood out. Eberle Winery makes a smooth, elegant Cabernet and Chardonnay, while Castoro Cellars to the south produces many different Zinfandels. One of the largest and most successful winemaking opera-tions in the Paso Robles area has been Meridian Vineyards, which aims at popular price levels.

The Edna Valley district south of the city of San Luis Obispo has several major producers. One of the most visible is Edna Valley Winery, aptly demonstrating the region's potential for Chardonnay. Corbett Canyon is a productive, well run

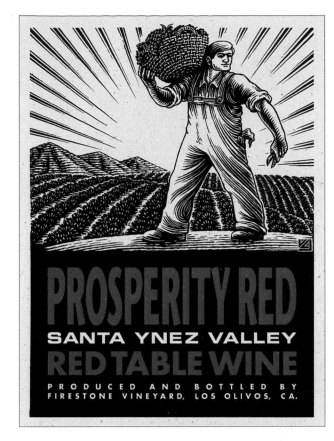

operation catering to the affordable price ranges. Further south at Arroyo Grande, Maison Deutz, owned by Champagne Deutz of France, is the largest sparkling wine producer in the area.

One of the showcases of the area is Cambria Winery & Vineyard, owned by Kendall-Jackson and an adjunct label for their immensely successful operation. Au Bon Climat, also in Santa Maria, is much sought after for their exciting Burgundian varietals – and an unusually good Pinot Blanc. Byron is famous for their Chardonnays. Zaca Mesa, one of the area's pioneer wineries has expanded their line to include many varietals from the Rhône in France.

Another early success was the Firestone Vineyard, established by tire producer Brooks Firestone in 1974 and soon a famous producer of Riesling (one of the state's first late-harvest Riesling specialists), Cabernet Sauvignon and Merlot.

One of the newest "stars" in the area is Fess Parker Winery, founded by actor Fess Parker in 1990 with son Eli Parker as winemaker. Sanford Winery in Buellton continues to make some outstanding Chardonnay and Pinot Noir. Their neighbor Mosby Winery at Vega has done extensive work with Italian varietals, while Sunstone Vineyards favors the

Rhône reds. Santa Barbara Winery, one of the area's first wineries, has some attractive flower labels but tends to be inconsistent.

❧ Central Valley ❧

The broad, fertile valley ranging from Sacramento in the north all the way to Bakersfield in the south is known as the Central Valley. It is one of the richest agricultural regions in California, and while wine grapes play a secondary role to table and raisin grapes in the Central Valley, they fill an important need in supplying the bulk wine producers that sustain California's reputation for quality everyday wines at an affordable price.

E. & J. Gallo, the nation's largest winery, makes its home in Modesto, where it churns out millions of cases a year of wines fitting every possible description; Heublein and Canandaigua's facilities elsewhere in the Valley are their major competition; recently R.H. Phillips has come upon the scene, furnishing wellmade varietals in the lower price categories. Bogle Vineyards in Clarksburg is another major player in the "fighting varietals" category; Château de Leu in Fairfield is similar. Further south, in the Manteca area, the Indelicato family have

been making wines for generations under the Delicato label.

Some of the state's foremost dessert wine producers make their home here. Ficklin is one of the oldest and most celebrated names in California port. Equally impressive is Andrew Quady's operation nearby: his select "Essencia," made from Orange Muscat, is a truly exceptional dessert wine.

❧ Sierra Foothills ❧

The foothills of the Sierra Nevada Mountains have turned into an important California wine region. The area became famous during the California gold rush of 1849, when growers discovered that other, more permanent riches lay in this fertile growing district. The Sierra Foothills area includes Amador County, the Nevada City district to the north, the city of Placerville and the Sonora area in Calaveras County – all told, a region extending some 70 miles, from north to south.

Because of the special soil and hot and dry growing season, the Sierra foothills are perfect for Zinfandel. Amador County Zins have become a legend in California: the wines are usually heady and potent with great complexity

Above: Movie star Fess Parker made history in the Santa Ynez Valley when he opened his new winery several years ago.

Left: Maison Deutz, of Champagne fame, now has important cellars in the Central Coast.

Above right: Once barrels have been used, they may still be refurbished for future vintages. Here is a team of coopers at work scraping the insides.

and outstanding flavors. Needless to say, White Zinfandels from many Amador County growers are among the best in the state. Cabernet Sauvignon and Sauvignon Blanc also do well in the region. Ports, sweet Muscats, and dessert wines are a specialty of many Sierra foothills wineries.

One of the best producers is Shenandoah Vineyards in Plymouth, established in 1977 by Leon and Shirley Sobon. Their Zinfandels are standard bearers. Montevina Wines is another excellent producer. Karly Wines in Plymouth is also a top producer, working with Rhône varietals and particularly rich Zinfandels. Amador Foothill Winery was one of the original wineries in the area. Renwood-Santino, makes Rhône varietals plus the usual robust Zinfandels. Other promising wineries include Charles Spinetta Winery, Charles B. Mitchell, Single Leaf, Terre Rouge, Vino Noceto, Windwalker and Latcham.

OREGON

Oregon rapidly became one of the most exciting American wine districts in the 1980s. For the first half of the century, many Oregon wineries grew mostly fruit and berry wines, but in recent years switched to high quality grapes. After many years of growing wine on a local basis, with only a few pioneers working hard to create an identity for Oregon wines, a combination of successful grapes and some superb vintages teamed up to put the state squarely on the nation's wine map.

One of the reasons for Oregon's huge success is its location. The climate is much cooler than California, and the growing season is longer. This means that grapes suited for the coolest climates are ideal for most Oregon wine regions. In recent years, the best vineyard locations have clearly been identified and expanded. Presently Oregon has over

100 bonded wineries, more than twice as many as recently as a decade ago.

The classic Burgundy varieties are garnering most of the attention in Oregon today. Chardonnay thrives in the cool environment, and Pinot Noir develops elegant fruit and complexity that recalls some of the best wines of the Côte d'Or. But a little known white Burgundy grape, Pinot Gris, has made a new niche for Oregon wines. It produces full, fragrant white wines that are now much in demand. Cabernet Sauvignon and Merlot are grown in select areas, mainly in the south, because the Oregon climate is a bit too cool for them. But the cool climate works to the advantage of Rieslings and Gewürztraminers, which are often exceptional in Oregon. Rivers are vital to Oregon vineyards. The Willamette River Valley defines an important wine district in Oregon. The riverine climate holds down temperature variations, and the soils are fertile and well drained.

Left: To many, Oregon vineyards represents the future for Pinot Noir in America. The Red Hills area is a prime example.

Right: Tualatin Vineyards was early to explore Oregon winegrowing. Their Yamhill cellars are a showpiece in the area.

Most of the traditionally famous Oregon producers lie just west of the city of Portland, in Yamhill County, where the climate and easy access to markets made the area an excellent choice. Better producers include Knudsen Erath, Cameron, Ponzi Vineyards, Rex Hill, Veritas Vineyard, Adelsheim Vineyard, Oak Knoll Winery, Sokol Blosser, Elk Cove, Amity Vineyards, Yamhill Valley Vineyards, Bethel Heights Vineyards, Tualatin Vineyards, and Shafer Vineyard Cellars. Most of these producers craft world-class Pinot Noir and Chardonnay, along with Pinot Gris.

In southern Oregon Forgeron Vineyard, Hinman, Hillcrest (a pioneer Oregon winery), Bjelland Vineyards, Bridgeview and Siskiyou Vineyards are all noted producers. More recently, Domaine Drouhin brought Veronique Drouhin's Burgundian winemaking expertise to the state, and noted California producers like Girard, William Hill and Pine Ridge have also set up additional wineries in Oregon.

WASHINGTON

Washington State is an agricultural paradise. A major percentage of the nation's apples and cherries are grown in the state, and it is only logical that wine grapes grow there too. But the Washington State wine industry was late in getting organized, and premium wine production only dates back to the late 1960s. The state's vintners have made incredible strides since then, and now over 75 Washington State wineries sell a wide array of quality products.

Unlike California and Oregon, which get regular rainfall from the Pacific Ocean, the Cascade Range blocks moisture and most of the inner agricultural districts in Washington State are hot and arid. Irrigation from the Columbia River basin is necessary for many vineyards. Winter frosts blowing down from Canada occasionally ravage the vines, which seldom occurs in the southern states. But in most years the warm, regular climate allows high quality wines to be made.

Very early on, growers determined that Cabernet Sauvignon and Merlot were well suited to the climate and soils in the state, and smooth, textured wines with soft tannins are a Washington State hallmark. For white wine varietals, Chardonnay and Sauvignon Blanc are also very successful.

The Yakima Valley to the north is traditionally the most famous wine district in Washington, benefiting from a protected location and a regular climate and rainfall pattern. Hogue Cellars in Prosser is a fine producer. Kiona Vineyards makes a particularly good Cabernet, and Covey Run (formerly Quail Run) excels at Chardonnay. Hinzerling Vineyards has been making good wines for years, and is now joined by more recent wineries like Blackwood Canyon, Stewart Vineyards and Tucker Cellars.

The Columbia River forms the border between Washington and Oregon, and also defines a major viticultural district. The river's presence, and its fertile, well-drained soils, play a vital part in the

ripening process. Three major wineries are headquartered here: Mount Elise Vineyards, Preston Wine Cellars and Bookwalter Winery in Pasco.

The Seattle area is home to several wineries that draw their grapes from outside sources. It is home to Washington's largest winery, Château Ste. Michelle. Its second moderately priced label, Columbia Crest, is deservedly popular. Columbia Winery, one of the oldest in the state, lies outside the capital in Bellevue; Paul Thomas Winery has already acquired an excellent following for its wines. Other notable producers in this area include E.B. Foote, Haviland Wines, and Vernier.

In the Puget Sound area, outside Seattle, several wineries have distinguished themselves. Quilceda Creek

Vintners makes a brilliant Cabernet Sauvignon, and Snoqualmie excels at white varieties. Mount Baker Vineyards and Manfred Vierthaler Winery are other good producers.

The Walla Walla district, in the southeastern corner of the state, is particularly noted for Cabernet. Leonetti Cellars makes an excellent example, as does Woodward Canyon. Finally, in the Spokane region to the north, Arbor Crest distinguishes themselves with their superior Merlots and Sauvignon Blancs, and Latah Creek and Worden's Washington Winery with their Chardonnays.

New York State

In the 1950s, vineyards in the northeast had only two alternatives: labrusca (the native American vine which has a "foxy" flavor – more suited for jam or juice than wine) or the French-American hybrids. Then Dr. Konstantin Frank, a Russian-born émigré to the Finger Lakes in New York, successfully demonstrated that vinifera vines grafted onto American root stock could be grown in cold climates as long as it was properly protected. The result has been a renaissance for northeastern vineyards.

The vinifera breakthrough has profoundly altered the nature of the New York Finger Lakes district. It firmly established the North Fork of Long Island as a top quality growing region, and led to new vineyards being founded in New Jersey, Connecticut, Pennsylvania and Virginia. Two centuries later, Thomas Jefferson's dream of northeastern American wine-growing has finally come true. New York is the second most important wine state after California. In 1996 the Empire State had over 35,000 acres of vineyards, which were traditionally centred in the Finger Lakes district, but vineyards were also expanding in the Hudson Valley district, Long Island's North Fork, and in the Chautauqua area near Lake Erie. They have responded to a general awareness in the state that New York can truly make great wine.

Much of New York is ideal for vineyards. The main limitation is the severe winters, when cold waves roaring down from Canada can devastate vines that are inadequately protected from frost. However modern frost protection measures have now been implemented. Today, New York vintners are beginning to recognize the uniqueness of several viticultural areas and are increasingly pairing the right grape varieties to specific soil and climate combinations.

Historically, the Finger Lakes region (Seneca, Cayuga, Keuka, Skaneateles) were the center of New York wine-growing. So named because they resemble the fingers of an outstretched hand, these massive lakes protect vineyards by moderating temperatures, and afford a microclimate of their own. The town of Hammondsport, on Lake Keuka, is the capital of the Finger Lakes vineyards, although Lake Seneca and Lake Cayuga have excellent wineries along their shores.

The biggest producer in the area is Canandaigua. The Taylor Wine Company in Hammondsport is one of their main labels; so is Great Western and Gold Seal, all traditional names in the New York wine industry. Walter S. Taylor, scion to the famous Taylor winemaking family, founded his own Bully Hill Winery in 1970 and spearheaded a move towards French hybrids. This maverick winemaker cum artist has contributed much to the industry, like his neighbor

Above left: Chateau St. Michelle's preeminence as Washington's largest producer may be gauged by this photo of cases ready for market.

Left: Chateau St. Michelle has several facilities. This one lies near the Columbia River, in the heart of Washington's prime vineyard area.

Right: Swedish Hill is an excellent winegrower in the Finger Lakes region of New York. David Whiting, their winemaker, samples a recent vintage.

Château Frank – now managed by Dr. Frank's son Willy Frank and continuing their excellent heritage of Pinot Noir, Johannisberg Riesling and Chardonnay. The smaller Heron Hill Winery sticks to white wine only.

Over in Dundee, Hermann Wiemer, originally from the Mosel district in Germany, was another early pioneer with vinifera grape varietals. His crisp, fruity Rieslings and sparkling wines recall his German winemaking heritage. His neighbor Glenora Cellars also sticks to vinifera grapes. McGregor Vineyard nearby produces light sprightly Rieslings.

Further east on Lake Seneca, Stanley (Bill) Wagner is famous for his Chardonnay and Riesling. Jim Doolittle's Frontenac Point Vineyard in Trumansburg has been a showcase since the early 1980s; Swedish Hill Cellars in Romulus is a consistent medal-winning winery, especially with their rich, textured late harvested wines.

Above: North Salem Vineyards, in northern Westchester County, NY, is often subject to harsh winters, but they have a regular production.

Left: The pioneers of Long Island viticulture, Alex and Louisa Hargrave, pictured here 20 years after they established their vineyards, with some of the many medals they have won for their wines.

Right: Bidwell Vineyards is another excellent producer on Long Island.

Long Island

Geologically, Long Island marks the limit of the glacial advances during the Ice Age. Most of the north shore is known technically as a terminal moraine; the sandy southern half lies on an outwash plain, and its famous barrier beaches face the Atlantic Ocean. Most of the outwash plain is heavily built up and otherwise unfit for vineyards, but on the North Fork there are some superb soils for vines. Many wineries have exploited them during the past decade, following the lead of Alex and Louisa Hargrave in 1973 when they were among the first to plant wine grapes.

Besides the soils, Long Island has important advantages over other wine regions in New York State. The ocean's warmth moderates winter temperatures, and devastating freezes that often ravage the vineyards upstate are unknown. The combination of regular sunshine, limited rainfall in summer and a warm, extended growing season provides an ideal environment for vinifera, which is reflected in the wines offered by most producers. Some of the state's best red wines are grown here, in comparison to northern vineyards that often do not get enough sun to develop the necessary color.

A number of small wineries did in fact exist in the North Fork beforehand, making some rather undistinguished wine from local labrusca varieties. Alex Har-

grave changed all that when he planted vinifera in his Cutchogue vineyard, specializing in red Bordeaux varieties (Cabernet Sauvignon, Merlot, Cabernet Franc). In less than a decade his wines were even winning awards in Bordeaux!

Following Hargrave's lead, Pugliese Vineyards, Bedell Vineyards, Peconic Bay Vineyards and Bidwell Vineyards all got their start in the area. Of this group, Bedell certainly stands out for their stylish Cabernets and Merlots; Bidwell is a larger operation that has recently made some sound wines. Peconic Bay makes a respectable Chardonnay; Pugliese is a well-run family operation that specializes in the Bordeaux varietals.

The biggest producer in the area is Pindar Vineyards, in Peconic Bay; they were established very early in the area and now enjoy a large share of the market. Their Merlot, and proprietary "Mythology" Meritage red, are especially good. Other excellent producers are Gristina Vineyards in Cutchogue and Lenz Winery, specializing in the classic Bordeaux varietals as well as Chardonnay. Over in Aquebogue, Robert Palmer

Left: Brotherhood, in the Hudson Valley, is New York's oldest winery – established in 1839.

Below: Benmarl Vineyards of Marlboro, NY, is another Hudson Valley pioneer – and a delight to visit in the fall.

Right: Oakencroft Vineyards in Virginia has an excellent reputation among northeastern winegrowers.

quickly made a name for himself with his excellent Chardonnays and Merlots. Paumanock Vineyards, also in Aquebogue, is a family-run operation crafting the same varieties.

The Hudson Valley

Grape vines have long graced the Hudson River Valley; in fact, America's oldest winery, Brotherhood, was founded in Washingtonville in 1839. In the 1960s, producer Everett Crosby moved into Rockland County and planted a vineyard atop a high ridge near Haverstraw named High Tor. The vines did well, but eventually Crosby had to close the winery. Following this lead, in 1971 Mark Miller moved to Marlboro in Ulster County and established Benmarl Vineyards. Both vintners were advised to grow French hybrids, as vinifera was considered risky for the climate of the Hudson Valley.

Miller's rapid fame led to others seeking the same opportunity. Across the river in Amenia, Bill Wetmore's Cascade Mountain Vineyards makes solid, rustic wines from local grapes; Clinton Vineyards, also in Dutchess County, quickly became known for their great Seyval Blancs (a French hybrid). Later on, politician John Dyson established a winery in Millbrook that quickly dispelled the notion that the Hudson Valley could not grow quality red vinifera.

Ulster County has also become an active vineyard area. One of the district's best Chardonnays is grown at West Park, overlooking former president Franklin D. Roosevelt's home across the river; Rivendell Winery in New Paltz is an aggressive producer with many good wines, although not all are home grown. Baldwin Vineyards in Pine Bush has made some lovely late harvest wines; Walker Valley Vineyards is another popular winery in the area.

Chautauqua & Lake Erie

The eastern shores of Lake Erie are an important vineyard area. The vines begin just south of Buffalo, and extend into nearby Pennsylvania and Ohio. The lake's warmth protects the vines from extreme winter cold, and they get regular rainfall. There are a few good producers in the area; Frederick S. Johnson in Westfield was one of the first, with their Johnson estate label. Merritt Estate in Forestville works with French hybrids, while Woodbury Vineyards in Dunkirk makes a respectable Chardonnay.

Left: Meredyth Vineyards was an early pioneer in Virginia winegrowing. Their success prompted dozens of others to follow.

Above and right: Fall Creek Vineyards is one of several top Texas wineries. Judging from recent efforts, the Lone Star State continues to stand tall.

VIRGINIA

The commonwealth of Virginia looks back proudly to the patronage of Thomas Jefferson, America's first wine authority, who hoped that the area around his residence at Monticello would one day be a great vineyard area. While the process took nearly two centuries, partly relating to the state's hesitant attitude towards alcoholic beverages, it has finally resulted in several dozen successful wineries, mainly surrounding the city of Charlottesville.

Virginia now has over 42 wineries, taking advantage of the warm climate and steady growing season throughout the state. Most of the wineries grow vinifera, although there are a few French-American hybrids in the northern part of the state. Chardonnay is a universal favorite among Virginia growers. The state's fondness for sweet wines affords opportunities for Riesling and Gewürztraminer in some areas, but only a few wineries produce Sauvignon Blanc or Pinot Gris. Among reds, Merlot is a clear favorite, reflecting current tastes, followed by Cabernet Sauvignon and Pinot Noir. Some of the better known Virginia wineries include Meredyth (one of the first), Oakencroft, Oasis, Barboursville, Naked Mountain, Prince Michel and Williamsburg.

TEXAS

The Lone Star State suddenly vaulted into the wine world in the 1980s. In response to a growing local demand for better wine; the state now has over 20 wineries, and new vineyards are constantly being planted. Unlike other mid- and southwestern wine-growing states, Texas has an ideal climate for vinifera.

The Texas panhandle is ideal for grapes because of a fairly consistent climate and low annual rainfall. Many acres of vines surround the area of Lubbock, and also further south near the capital city of Austin. The state's largest producer, Ste. Genevieve, is located at Fort Stockton and is now owned by Cordier s.a. of France; Slaughter Leftwich Vineyards and Fall Creek Vineyards in Austin; Pheasant Ridge Winery and Llano Estacado Winery in Lubbock; and Messina Hof Winery in Bryan were early Texas wineries and now contribute much of the production.

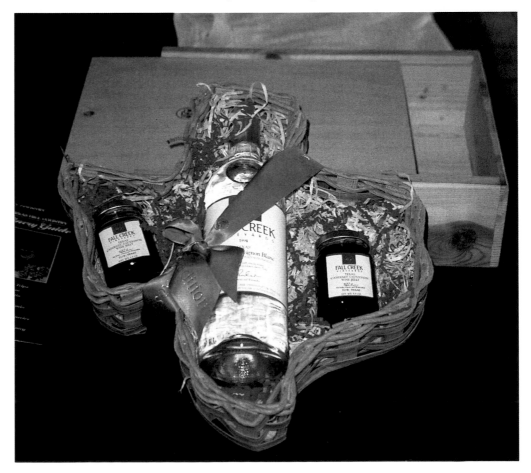

CHILE

In less than ten years, Chile has become America's third largest wine exporter. Production costs are relatively low, making many of the wines quite reasonably priced. Also, because many of the wines are sold as "varietals" (by the name of the informing grape variety), they are instantly familiar to American and British buyers. Finally, because Chileans like to buy wines they can enjoy right away, these wines are usually ready to drink at the time of purchase.

The principal red grape variety in Chile is Cabernet Sauvignon. Depending on where they are grown, Chilean Cabernet Sauvignons are somewhat softer and rounder than their American or French counterparts, reflecting winemaking and consumer preferences. Merlot is another key variety; it makes excellent wines and is often blended with Cabernet. Among white varieties, Sauvignon Blanc and Sémillon are popular, similar in style to white Bordeaux; Chardonnay is relatively new to many Chilean vineyards and consequently is in the process of establishing its own identity.

Located in the country's temperate zone, mostly around the capital city of Santiago, Chile's vineyards enjoy several distinct advantages. Protected from the cool Pacific Ocean by a series of coastal mountain ranges called cordilleras, and then by the towering Andes Mountains to the east, wine grapes flourish in a prolific area several hundred miles long, where rainfall and sunshine are remarkably consistent.

Traditionally the Maipo River Valley, which flows near the city of Santiago, had the best combination of climate and

soil for wine grape growing. The first vineyards were established in this area in the sixteenth century, at the time of Spanish colonial settlement. As Santiago's population expands, more vintners have turned to the north and south of Santiago. Many of the biggest wineries grow their grapes in Lontue, Rancagua, Rapel and Maule to the south, where it is somewhat cooler, and in particular the Colchagua Valley in the Maule district. A well-publicized investment in 1988 of the Los Vascos Winery, by Domaines Rothschild of France, highlighted this new international interest in Chile's wine-growing potential.

Over half of all Chilean wine exports are furnished by a single, giant producer: Concha y Toro, which also has a second label, Walnut Crest, further contributing to its sales. This producer dominates the market by virtue of its outstanding value for money.

Dozens of smaller wineries comprise

the remainder of Chilean exports. Estates with a long-standing tradition include Cousino Macul of Santiago, in the Cousino family for generations since 1856; Santa Rita, also of Santiago, which is widely distributed in Chile; Undurraga, a venerable label with a new look and a new level of quality; and some newer players like Caliterra, Santa Carolina, Canepa, Carmen, St. Morillon, Carta Vieja, Santa Monica, and Valdivieso – the latter has a fine new Stone Lake label. All of these are reliable brands and almost all are excellent value.

Left: Dramatic view of Viña Aquitania, outside Santiago, Chile.

Above right: St. Morillon is a popular label distributed by Mitjans of Santiago, Chile. Here is Luis Simian, their winemaker.

Above: Getting around on horseback is still an effective means of transportation in Chilean vineyards.

Right: Harvest at Carmen Vineyards, in the Maipo Valley, Chile. They have recently expanded their Chardonnay production.

ARGENTINA

Located on the eastern flank of the Andes Mountains, which separates her from her neighbor Chile, Argentina's vineyards have been famous for centuries. The industry is now in the midst of some pro-found changes, affecting the quality and the price of many wines, and despite many adjust-ments in the cellars, the prospects are encouraging.

If a single word could characterize the Argentine wine industry, it would be: overproduction. Prolific grape varieties are planted in irrigated fertile soils in a highly productive climate. The result has been a glut of light, uninteresting wines sold at very low prices. After many decades of producing this type of wine, many Argentine growers are slowly cut-ting back on yields and selecting better grape varieties.

Spanish settlers brought the first cut-tings to Argentina, and the Spanish mis-sions were the first to appreciate the country's homegrown wines. Cattle ranching brought many immigrants to Argentina in the hopes of starting a new life. A large number of these were Ital-ians, who were familiar with wine-grow-ing in their home country and found con-ditions in Argentina to be ideal.

For this reason, many of the first grapes to become popular had Italian ori-gins. Barbera and Nebbiolo originally came from Piedmont, and in Argentina's mild climate they produce similar wines; Malbec (often spelled Malbeck), from

Left: Weinert Cellars in Mendoza, is one of the premium wine producers in Argentina.

Right: Workers at the Catena Winery, a part of Bodegas Esmeralda in Argentina. This winery creates a particularly fine Chardonnay and Cabernet Sauvignon under the direction of Paul Hobbs.

the Bordeaux district, gives rich red wines with a characteristic flavor. More recently, the best red wines have been made with Cabernet Sauvignon and Merlot – either by themselves or in blends. White wines have traditionally played a secondary role to the reds. Chenin Blanc, is popular with many growers, as is Sauvignon Blanc. Chardonnay is a more recent varietal, but it has the greatest quality potential.

Much of the land west of the city of Buenos Aires is ideal for vineyards, but particularly in the area around Mendoza, where the land begins to rise up and meet the Andes, the best climates and soils are found. The area of San Rafael south of Mendoza is cooler and hence is better for table wines; the San Juan region to the north grows grapes primarily for brandies and fortified wines. Irrigation is required because rainfall is usually blocked by the towering Andes. But snow melt is sufficient to make up the water deficit.

The biggest winery in the nation is Penaflor, which sells under the Trapiche label, but in recent years a number of smaller producers have started to export their wines. Bodegas Norton and Umberto Canale in the Rio Negro area have a distinguished history. In Mendoza, Navarro Correas Bodegas Etchart, and Finca Flichman (with their top label Caballero de la Cepa) are all reliable pro-

Left: Pedro Luis Manchevsky, of Bodegas Esmeralda, sampling a recent vintage.

Below: Some of the Malbec reserve at Penaflor/Trapiche Winery in Mendoza.

Above right: John Duval, chief winemaker at Penfolds Wines in Australia, inspecting his vines.

Below right: At Penfolds' Clare Valley estate, these Chardonnay vines are organically grown – as can be seen by the vegetation at the foot of the vines.

ducers; Valentin Bianchi in San Rafael and Pasqual Toso in San Jose make a wide range of good wines.

Some of the most exciting wines in Argentina have been produced by Bodegas Weinert, whose smooth, Bordeaux-styled Cabernet Sauvignon is much in demand; and Bodegas Esmeralda in Mendoza, where the American winemaker Paul Hobbs was recently hired to craft premium Chardonnay, Cabernet Sauvignon and Malbec for the Catena label.

AUSTRALIA

Australia has rapidly become one of the world's foremost wine producers. The wines are well-suited to British and American markets because they are made from familiar grape varieties and bear names that are easy to pronounce. Most important, they are apt to be quite consistent.

The industry originally grew fortified wines (ports, sherries), and table wine production expanded slowly. But in the two centuries that followed the official beginning of the Australian wine industry in 1788, wine districts were clearly mapped out and the stage was set for quality wine production.

There are no indigenous grape varieties in Australia; like most other countries in the New World, they had to be brought from Europe. Almost all grapes thrive in the sunny climate; however, there has been a major move recently to match particular varieties with the right soil and growing areas, with the result that some varietals have surged ahead in quality.

A prime example is Chardonnay, which was almost unknown in Australia twenty years ago, to the extent that most "white burgundy" sold in Australia was made from Sémillon, not from Chardonnay. Now it is planted all over the country. A generation ago many vineyards were also planted in Sylvaner, but have now been turned over to better varieties like Chardonnay and Sauvignon Blanc. True Riesling, referred to as Rhine Riesling or White Riesling, is grown on a limited basis, but it can produce very attractive semi-dry wines and even better late-harvested wines, when the conditions are right. Sémillon on its own gives a round, full white wine; a number of producers blend it with Chardonnay for added complexity and call it "Sem/Chard." Very often, these blends are better wines than they would be separately and are quite popular.

Australia's prototypical red variety is Syrah, also known as Shiraz, which gives solid, substantial red wines with plenty of fruit and extract. It is often mixed with Cabernet Sauvignon to give additional structure and complexity; on its own, Cabernet Sauvignon makes some of Australia's best red wines, in a variety of different styles. Merlot is sometimes seen, often in blends with Cabernet Sauvignon, but it is not always easy to grow in warm climates. Pinot Noir, when matched with the right soils, can give excellent results.

Fortified wines like port and sherry were Australia's first wines, and they nurtured an entire older generation of wine drinkers. Although they are now less important than they once were, Australian fortified wines still rank with some of the world's best. For ports, Australian vintners usually choose Cabernet Sauvignon or, less frequently, Shiraz.

The Australian wine business first developed from vineyards planted near the city of Sydney but as the population

grew in the rest of the country, new wine regions were founded. The suburbs of Adelaide were already famous wine districts by the 1840s, and in New South Wales the glorious Hunter River Valley was planted about the same time. In western Australia, one of the best of these regions, the Margaret River district south of the city of Perth, has only recently been explored.

The Hunter Valley has one of the world's best combinations of climate, rainfall and soil, to the extent that some of Australia's most famous wineries are located there. Two Hunter Valley wineries stand out: Tyrrell's Wines, where pioneer Murray Tyrrell was the first to plant Chardonnay in the Hunter Valley in 1962 and prove it could produce world-class wines; and Rosemount Cellars, which pioneered the rich, textured style of Chardonnay in their Roxburgh and "Show Reserve" series. Although the top wines from these wineries are all rather costly, they also have a full range of wines in the more affordable categories.

Other distinguished Hunter Valley wineries include McWilliams (also at Riverina); Lindemans, who developed important vineyards in the Padthaway district; Evans Family, spearheaded by Len Evans, a great promoter of Australian wines; Lake's Folly, whose splendid Cabernets have proved to be anything but; and Rothbury Estate, a traditional producer. Wyndham Estate at Branxton is a major winery associated with the Saxonvale, Hunter Estate and Richmond Grove labels.

The Mudgee area northwest of Sydney has seen the growth of several new wineries. Montrose and Craigmoor are popular labels here. Huntington Estate is another highly regarded Mudgee producer. Victoria to the south has many important wine districts. The Rutherglen region recently came into prominence; another excellent region is Bendigo/Ballarat, where several wineries (Balgownie Wines, Yellowglen) are situated. Brown Brothers in Milawa is one of the state's best known table wine producers, and Stanton & Killeen make some of the best fortified wines in the nation. Château Tahbilk in the Goulbourn area is a well known producer.

The region surrounding Adelaide is another traditional wine area. Wynn's Cellars pioneered the Coonawarra district over a century ago, and their rich, refined Cabernets are much in demand today. Seppelt, Mildara and Katnook all make superb wines. The Barossa Valley north of Adelaide contains many of Australia's most important wineries. Penfolds, where the late Max Shubert, their legendary winemaker, perfected the famous Grange Hermitage Cabernet/Shiraz blends, is a superb producer; Hardy's, one of the nation's biggest wineries, has an excellent array of wines at many different price levels; Orlando (Gramp's) is another major producer, noted for their affordable, consistent Jacob's Creek Claret. Krondorf makes some excellent wines; Peter Lehmann is another label associated with good value. Henschke Winery is noted for their striking label and equally striking wines; "Kaiser Stuhl" is famous for their Rieslings. Saltram Winery has made some excellent varietals in recent years. Finally, Yalumba Winery, owned by Smith & Sons, makes

Left: Rosemount Shiraz – with currants and cherries as a backdrop, alluding to the flavors the wine offers.

Right: Rosemount Chardonnay – with a plethora of fruit descriptors.

some outstanding ports in addition to table wines, and also markets the Hill-Smith estate and Heggies labels.

The Adelaide Hills district, to the north of the city, saw a great expansion of vineyards in the 1980s. One of the most visible of the new wineries was Petaluma, whose wines often synthesized European styles with a clear Australian identity. In the Southern Vales district to the south of Adelaide, Château Reynella makes excellent port, good varietals and adequate sparkling wine; Wirra Wirra is another noted producer. Clare Watervale completes the list of Adelaide wine regions; Mitchell's is a good label, along with Stanley Leasingham, whose Cabernet/Shiraz blends can be excellent.

In western Australia, the Swan Valley was the original source of winemaking in the area. Houghton Winery was an early triumph, along with Paul Conti and Sandalford. Now the Margaret River district south of the city of Perth is an area that is creating new excitement, particularly for Cabernet Sauvignon and Chardonnay. Vasse Felix was one of the first wineries to win awards in international competition; today, Cullens, Leeuwin Estate and Moss Wood have all added to the region's reputation for producing prime quality Cabernet Sauvignon.

Above: Bruce Tyrrell, of Tyrrell's Winery in Australia, sampling some of his wares.

Left: Château Tahbilk in the Goulbourn area of Australia is a well known producer as well as an historical landmark.

Right: Workers at a vineyard in New Zealand.

NEW ZEALAND

Founded in 1820, New Zealand's wine industry grew at a relatively slow pace until the 1970s, when a surge in new vineyards – combined with a new public demand for better wines – put New Zealand winegrowers in a new position. A surplus of wine then resulted, which turned out to be a mixed blessing because much of it was ordinary wine, poorly suited either to export or the home market. The solution was a readjustment to new grape varieties, a curtailment of vineyards that were producing too much, and a new focus on exports. The results paid off handsomely: New Zealand wines have performed splendidly at international competitions.

So far, the most successful white grape variety seems to be Sauvignon Blanc, which thrives in New Zealand's temperate climate and adapts well to a wide variety of soils. Vinified dry, it gives very scented and fruity white wines that have been well received. Chardonnay has also been successful, although perhaps not to the same degree; the wines are often a bit light to sustain the sort of oak winemakers have been subjecting them to. On a smaller scale, varieties like White Riesling and Gewürztraminer have been quite successful.

The relatively cool climate in most of the country dictated that red wines take a back seat to the racy, scented whites, but some New Zealand reds made during the last decade have been truly excellent. Most of them have been produced from Cabernet Sauvignon, here as in Australia

the preferred choice for a claret-styled wine; recently Merlot has entered on the scene, either as a valuable blending grape or on its own as a varietal. There are also a few good New Zealand Pinot Noirs.

New Zealand's first vineyards were planted around Auckland. As the population slowly expanded southwards in search of more land for vineyards, new wine areas sprang up. The major wine-growing regions now include Hawke's Bay, along the southeastern coast; Gisborne, further inland, Matawhero, west of Gisborne; Henderson, along the northeastern coast, and Poverty Bay – an unfortunate name for an area that has recently bestowed riches on some of its better winegrowers.

By the 1950s a dozen recognized viticultural areas were in place on North Island, forming a large semicircle beginning at Auckland and ending just to the east of Wellington, the capital. South Island, it was believed, was simply too cold for good vineyards. All that changed when two of the biggest New Zealand wine companies, Montana Wines Ltd. and Corbans, surveyed available land on South Island and planted thousands of acres of vineyard there, chiefly in the dis-

Below: Spectacular scenery at Fromm Winery in the Marlborough district of New Zealand.

Right: Te Mata Estate on North Island, New Zealand – one of the most famous producers of Cabernet Sauvignon in the country.

WAIRAU RIVER
1993

SAUVIGNON BLANC
MARLBOROUGH
e750ml   12.0% Vol.
WINE OF NEW ZEALAND
Produced and Bottled by Wairau
River Wines, RD3 Blenheim, N.Z.

trict of Marlborough. The results are most impressive with Sauvignon Blanc and Chardonnay.

Besides major producers like Montana and Corbans, New Zealand has dozens of select growers who are committed to export and maintain the highest production standards. One of the most remarkable of these is Te Mahta of Auckland, whose rare, pricey red wine called Coloraine is frequently among the country's best. Kumeu River, Cooper's Creek, Selaks and Babich Wines are all reliable labels. Cloudy Bay of South Island has recently gained a lot of press as one of New Zealand's select producers, as has its neighbor Villa Maria in Marlborough. Goldwater Estate, located near Auckland but with vineyards on South Island, has made some expensive but exceptional wines lately.

SOUTH AFRICA

When the restrictive governmental policy of apartheid officially ended in 1993, it represented a new beginning for the South African economy, which experienced a spectacular recovery in the 1990s. Actually, fine wines have been grown in South Africa for over 400 years, since Dutch settlers first brought vine cuttings to the region near Capetown and officially established the wine industry.

Production expanded rapidly during the nineteenth century, to the extent that by the First World War, many wineries were producing a surplus. It was this surplus, and a desire to control wine production and standardize it under a few famous labels, that led to the growth of cooperative cellars in South Africa. Because so many growers belong to the cooperatives, there has only been a recent trend for smaller producers to bottle their wine themselves, but with improved trading prospects this is happening at a much more rapid rate than before.

With only a few exceptions, South Africa grows most of the familiar varieties associated with French, German and Italian wines, and adds a few of her own. In the traditional styles, South Africa's most prolific white variety is Steen, said to be a clone of Chenin Blanc and South African Riesling which make

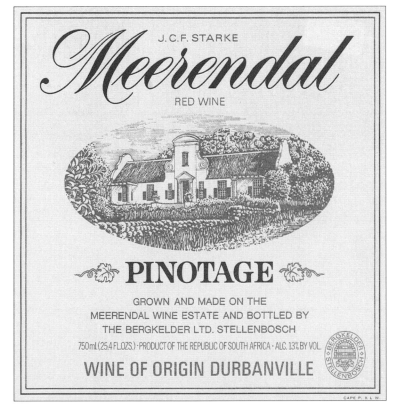

Opposite top: As the sign says, Gisborne is a major Chardonnay producing region in New Zealand.

Opposite bottom: Vineyards of the Cooper's Creek Winery in the Auckland district.

Below: Harvest time at vineyards in Paarl, South Africa.

Left: Cathedral Cellar of the KWV Wine Estate in South Africa is one of the nation's largest producers.

Below: Klein Constantia, a wine that recalls South Africa's proud wine-growing heritage.

Right: Harvest in a South African vineyard.

adequate carafe wine. Colombard (French Colombard) is also a valuable blending grape, best for dry white wines since it has a characteristic high acidity and fresh, fruity flavor.

An excellent, rather underrated red South African grape is Pinotage, a blend of Pinot Noir and Cinsault that is unique to the country. Normally it gives wines with plenty of color and a rich, spicy flavor. Cinsault (spelled Cinsaut in South Africa) is grown for much of the country's ordinary bulk wine, but on its own as a varietal it can sometimes give quite excellent results.

It is a newer breed of wines from private resources, though, that will firmly establish South Africa's reputation on the international wine market. Some of the best results have come from Chardonnay. A whole new attitude towards high quality, dry wines has prompted many producers to plant it. Another superior grape is Sauvignon Blanc, which as in France gives several different types of wine depending on whether it is barrel-aged.

Many of the country's best red wines have been made from Cabernet Sauvignon, especially when aged in French oak and matured in the Bordeaux style. Either by itself, or in blends with Merlot, South African Cabernets have distinguished themselves at many international judgings. Efforts at growing Pinot Noir have been less successful.

The South African wine industry was originally established for port, sherry and brandy production. For this reason, thousands of acres were planted in ordinary varieties, such as the Little Karoo district, where quantity was more important than quality. Because of the consistent climate, many South African fortified wines and brandies were of excellent quality. Table wines, on the other hand, only became important much later because of their different location and production requirements.

In the early nineteenth century, a noted estate near Capetown made a superb fortified Muscat wine called Constantia, which graced many a Victorian table. While this historic wine is no longer made, the original estate still survives under government ownership, and is known as Groot Constantia. A number of good table wines are also produced there today.

North of Capetown, some of the country's best vineyard acreage is located at Paarl, now an officially delimited wine district, and also east of Capetown at Stellenbosch. The Kooperatieve Wijnbouwers Vereiniging is Paarl's biggest producer, and the Stellenbosch Farmer's Winery, South Africa's second largest winery, controls several popular labels such as Zonnebloem and Niederburg. Boschendal has become famous for their clean, fresh white wines. Bergkelder is another famous cellar in Stellenbosch, controlling the popular Fleur du Cap and Grunberger labels that have done well on the export market.

Smaller, newer wineries are supplementing these traditional labels as table wines move ahead. Besides the bigger cooperatives, the Stellenbosch region includes producers like Rustenberg, Thelema Mountain Vineyards, Blaawklippen, Alto, Le Bonheur, Delheim, Hartenberg, Hazendal, Meerlust and Kanonkop. In acknowledgement of Constantia's great fame, a new winery, Klein Constantia, has made some very fine wines near Capetown.

CLASSIC FOOD & WINE PAIRINGS

Food	Wine
Hors D'oeuvres	Champagne, sparkling wine, Chardonnay
Raw vegetables	Pinot Grigio, Chenin Blanc
Nuts	Dry Fino Sherry or Amontillado; Sercial Madeira
Shellfish (raw)	Champagne, Chablis, Muscadet, Vinho Verde
Soups (clear)	Dry Fino Sherry or Amontillado; Sercial Madeira
Soups (cream base)	Chardonnay, any dry white
Soups (thick)	Pinot Noir, any dry red
Cold cuts & poultry	White Zinfandel or semi-dry rosé
Meat & poultry with Barbecue sauce	Red Zinfandel, Syrah, Côtes-du-Rhône
Bouillabaisse	Chardonnay or dry rosé
Fish (baked, grilled)	Chardonnay, Pouilly-Fuissé
Chicken & turkey	Pinot Noir, Beaujolais or Chardonnay (with white meat)
Pork & ham	Chenin Blanc, White Zinfandel, Rhine or Mosel of Kabinett to Spätlese quality
Veal	Pinot Noir, Rioja, or any other light red
Lamb	Cabernet Sauvignon or Merlot
Roast beef	Pinot Noir, Beaujolais or Côtes-du-Rhône
Steak	Cabernet Sauvignon or Syrah
Stews	Zinfandel, Côtes-du-Rhône, Beaujolais
Game	Full-bodied Rhône reds (Hermitage, Châteauneuf du Pape) Barolo, Petite Sirah
Salad	No wine (vinegar dressing spoils it)
Cheese	Surprisingly, not all wines enhance the flavor of cheese. Here are some good combinations: Cow's milk: any full bodied red Goat: any dry white Roquefort: Sauternes or other sweet white Stilton: Ruby, LBV or Vintage Port Gorgonzola & strong blues: Amarone, Barolo, Barbaresco
Dessert	Sauternes, Vouvray, Moscato d'Asti, Auslesen, other late-harvested wines

Above: Beet soup and a bottle of rosé. The combination can't be beat.

Below left: A feast at one of Sicily's top wine estates, Regaleali, where chef Mario Lorenzo and Anna Tasca assemble a bountiful crop.

Below right: Bidwell Vineyards on Long Island serves their recent vintages of white wine with a lobster dinner.

Right: In Burgundy, even a simple chicken dish becomes a feast when dressed with vegetables of the season and served with wines from the Côte Chalonnaise.

INDEX

Photo Credits

Austrian Wine Office: 131, 132, 132-133.
Bidwell Vineyards: 167, 188(bottom right).
Bonny Doon Vineyards: 157.
Cain Vineyard and Winery: 148(bottom).
Champagne Wines Information Bureau: 61(top), 62(top).
Chateau Tahbilk: 181(left).
Cyprus Embassy Trade Center: 126, 127.
Gerry Dawes: 8, 9, 11(top right), 14, 16(top), 18(top), 19(top left), 21, 32, 34(bottom), 39, 40(top), 58(top), 61(bottom), 62(bottom), 63(top), 65, 66(top), 70(bottom), 71, 73, 74, 75,

76, 77, 78, 79(top), 80(right), 94, 102, 103, 116, 118, 119, 121, 123, 124(bottom), 145(bottom), 156, 158(bottom), 160(top), 162, 171(top).
Foods and Wines from France, Inc.: 189.
German Wine Information Bureau: 20, 89, 91.
Kobrand, Inc.: 113, 115(top).
Maison Deutz: 160(bottom).
Sara Matthews: 1, 2, 3, 6, 7, 10, 10-11, 11(top left), 12, 13, 15, 16(bottom), 17, 22, 30-31, 33(top), 34(top), 37(top), 38, 41, 43(bottom), 45, 47, 48(top), 49, 50, 51(top), 52(top), 54(top), 56(top left), 56-57, 59, 60, 63(bottom), 68, 69, 70(top), 72, 92, 93(bottom), 95(top), 96, 97,

99, 100, 101, 104(top), 105, 117, 120, 128, 136(bottom), 137(bottom), 166(bottom), 170, 171(bottom), 172, 173, 174, 175, 176.
New Zealand Trade Development Board: 135, 180(bottom), 183(inset), 184(top).
Oakencroft Vineyard & Winery: 169.
Opus One: 147.
Palace Brands, Inc.: 93(top), 106(top).
Riedel Crystal: 29.
Rosemount Estates: 178, 179.
Rubin/Hunter Communications: 177.
South African Tourism Board: 112, 185, 186, 187.
Maguerite Thomas: 28, 33(bottom), 36, 37(bottom), 40(bottom), 42(bottom), 44, 52(bottom), 53,

54(bottom), 55(top), 58(bottom), 64, 66-67, 67(top), 79(bottom), 80(left), 82, 83, 85, 86, 91(bottom), 107, 108, 109, 122, 124(top), 125, 129, 130, 151, 152, 153, 155, 165, 188(top), 188(bottom left).
Vine Ventures International, Inc.: 138, 139.
Tom Wanstall: 4-5, 18-19, 19(top right), 26(bottom), 140, 141, 142, 143, 144, 145(top), 146, 148(top), 149(top), 150, 154, 161, 163, 164, 166(top), 168.
Winebow, Inc.: 98, 180(top).
The Wine Enthusiast: 23, 24, 25, 26(top), 27.
Wine Institute of New Zealand: 184(bottom); Steven Morris: 182-183.
York Mountain Winery: 159(right).